Color Book
A Colorful Journey

Have a look at the books
in our catalogue

https://linktr.ee/vibrantvistas

Track your progress

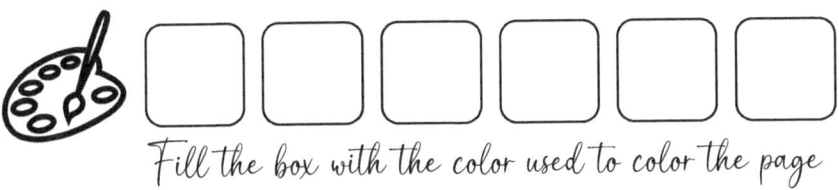

Fill the box with the color used to color the page

Write the day when you started coloring this page

Write how much time it took you to complete

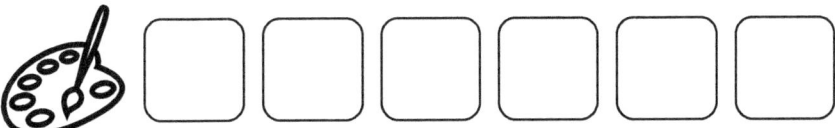

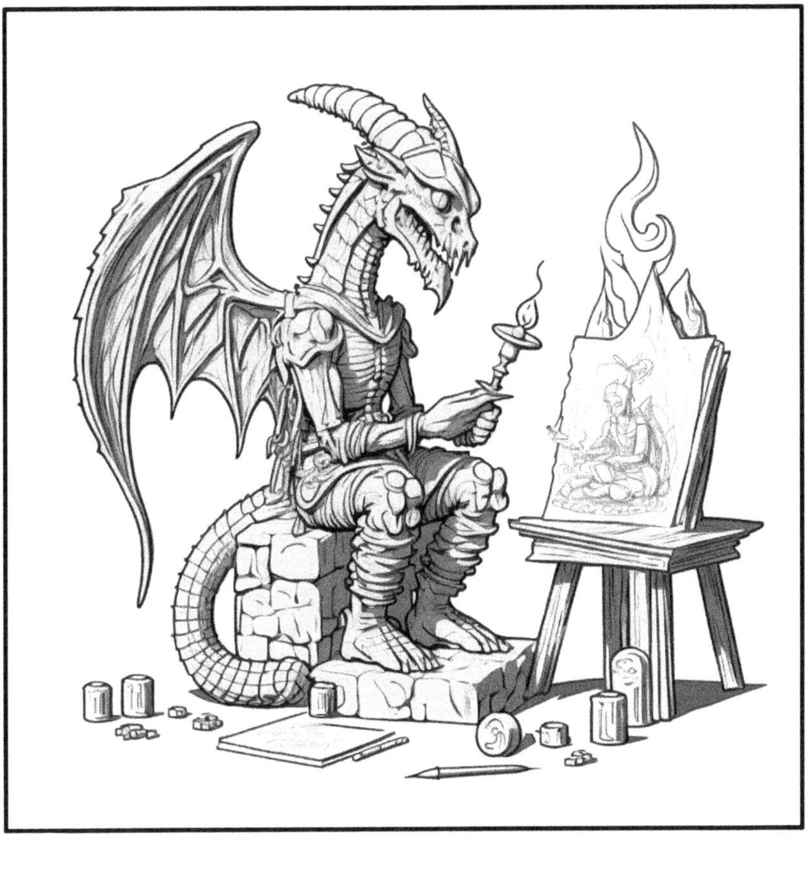

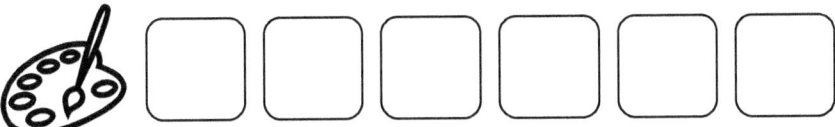

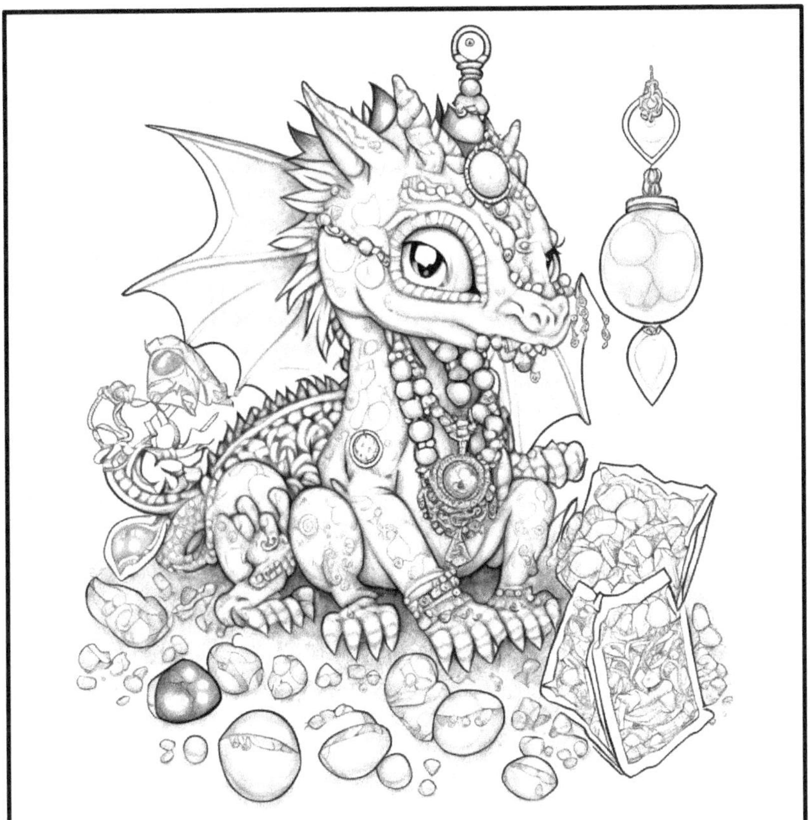

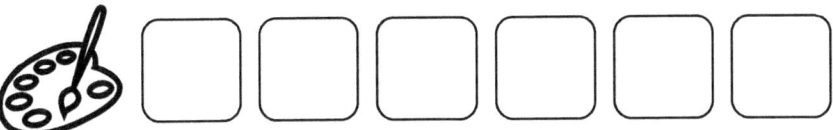

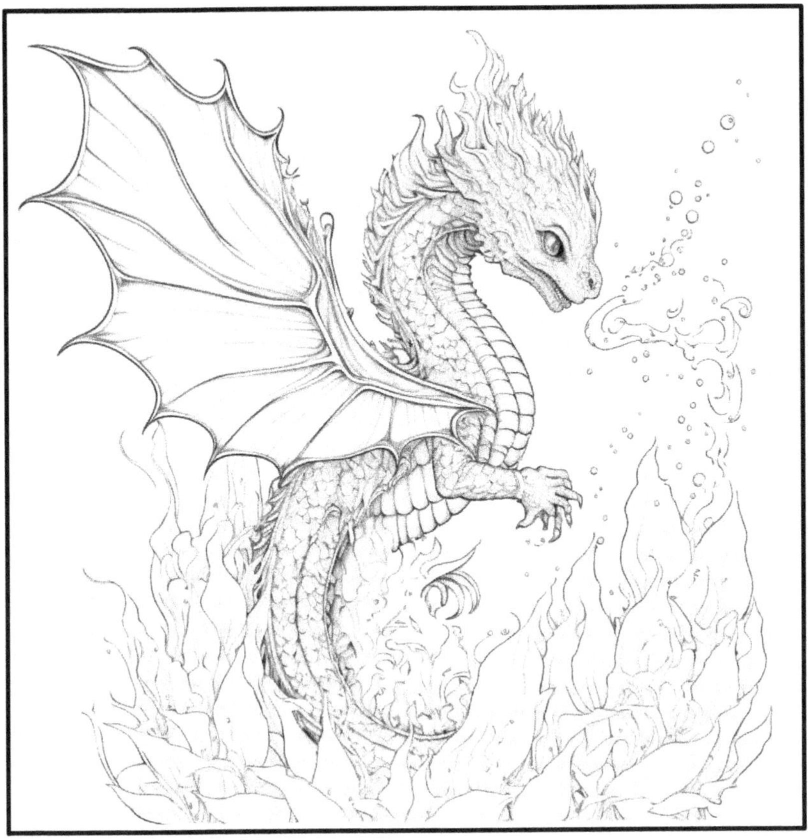

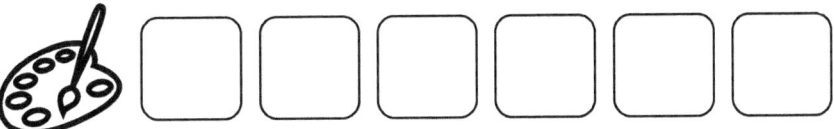

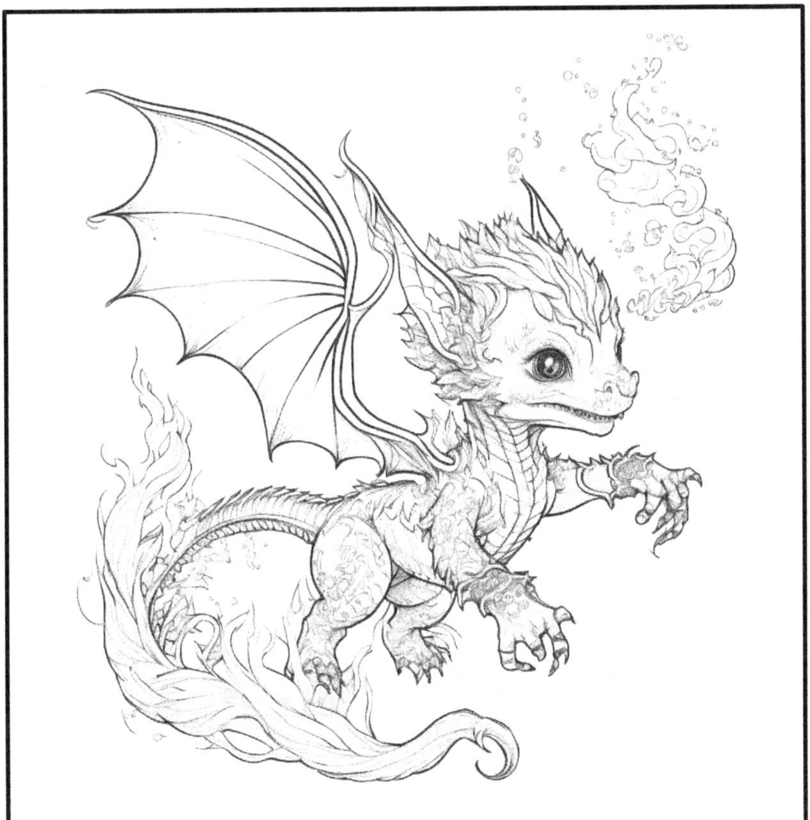

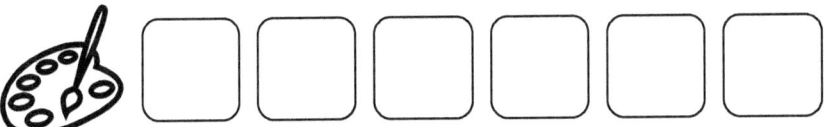

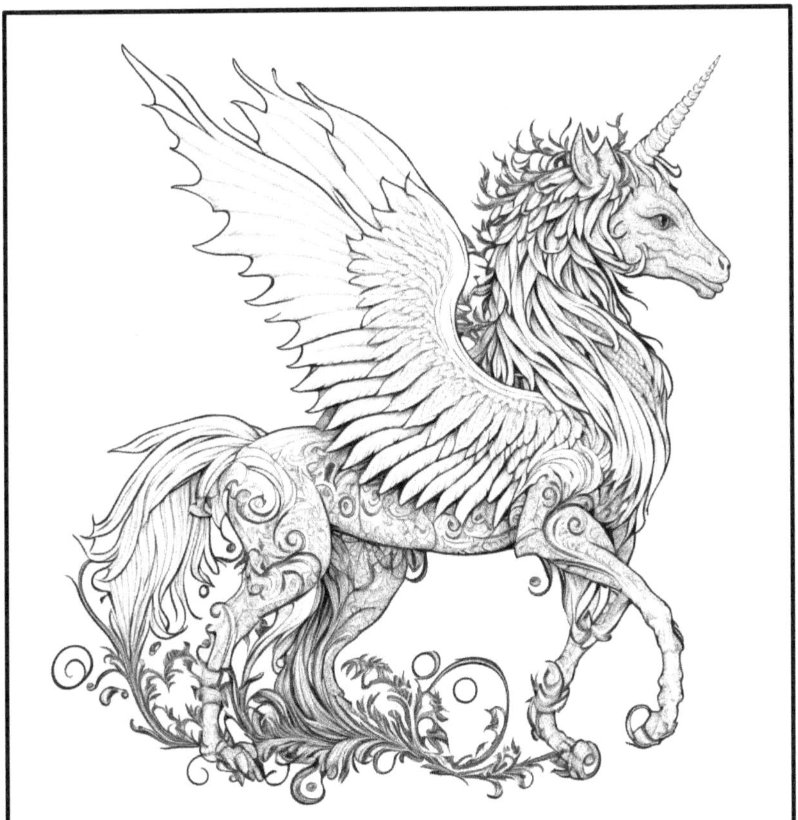

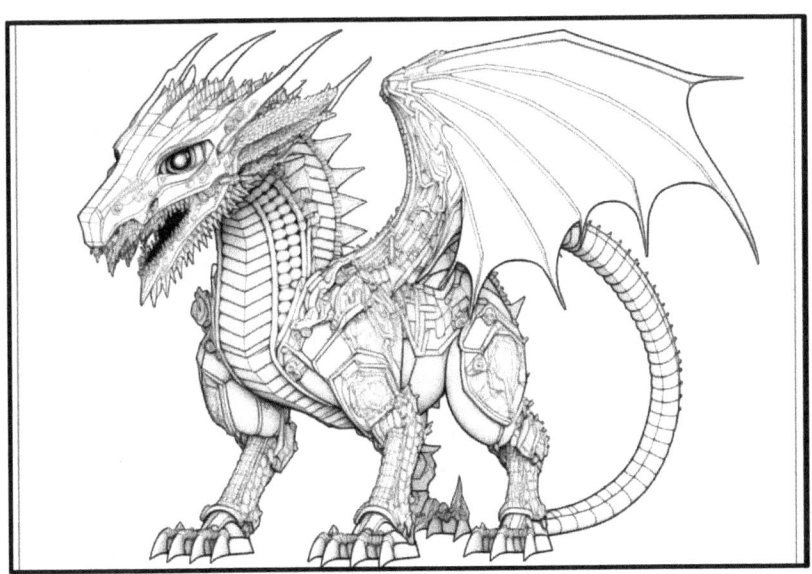

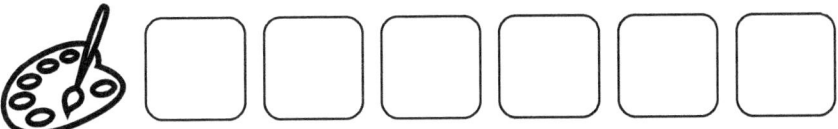

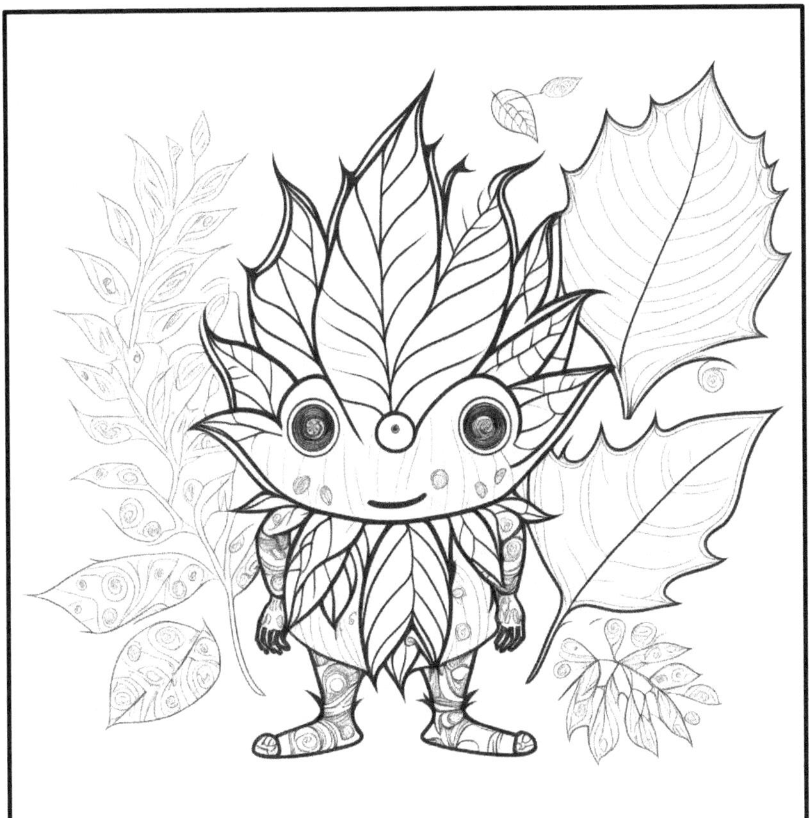

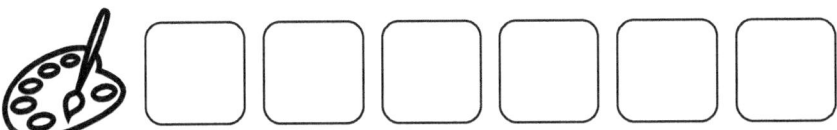

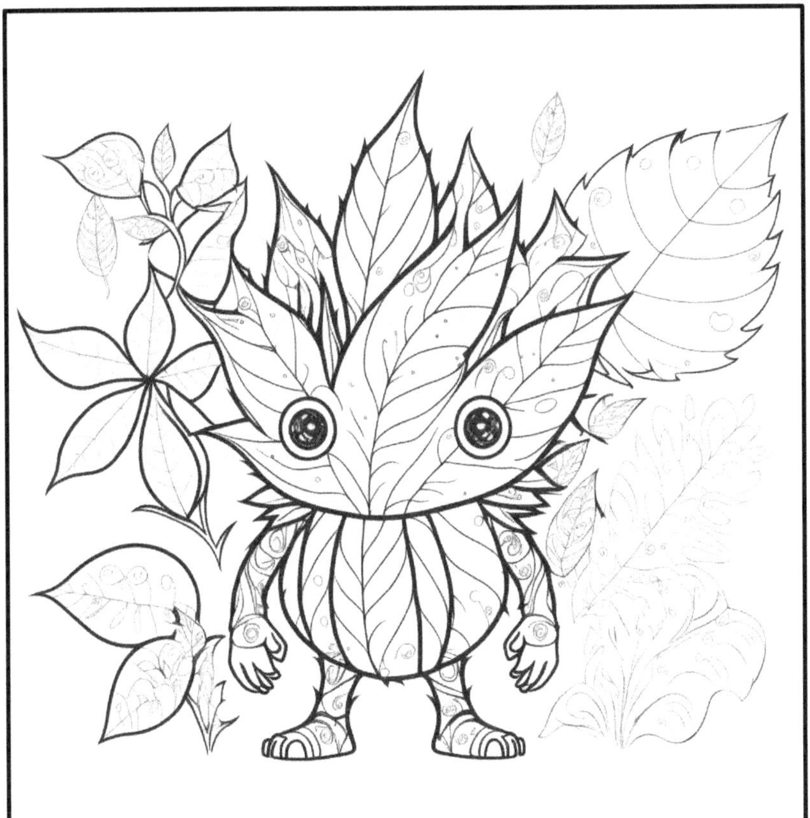

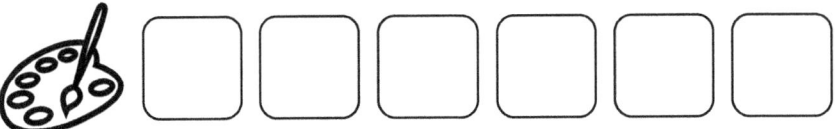

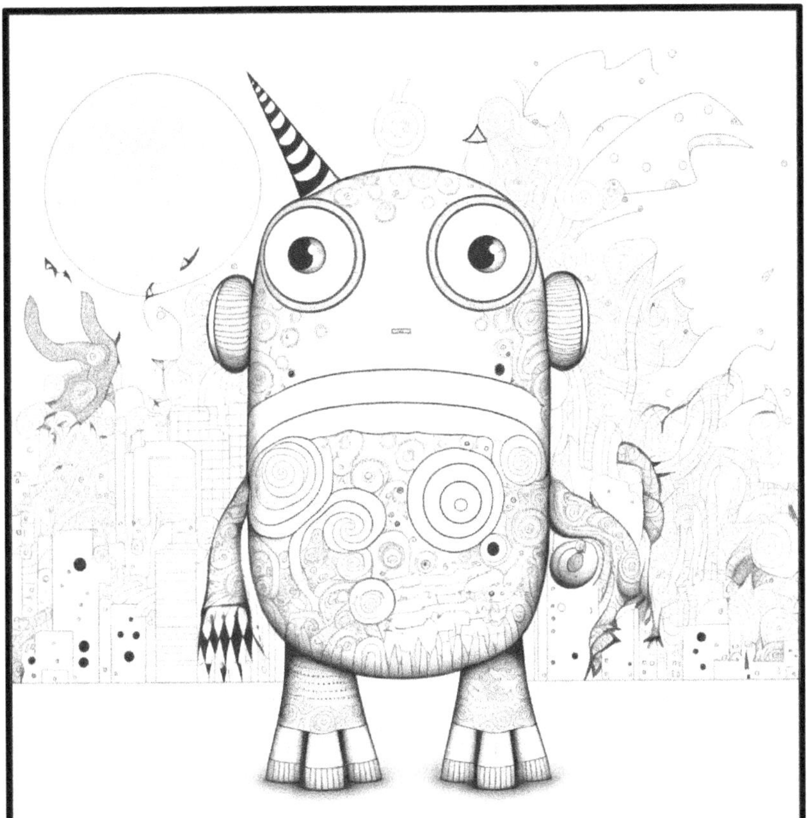

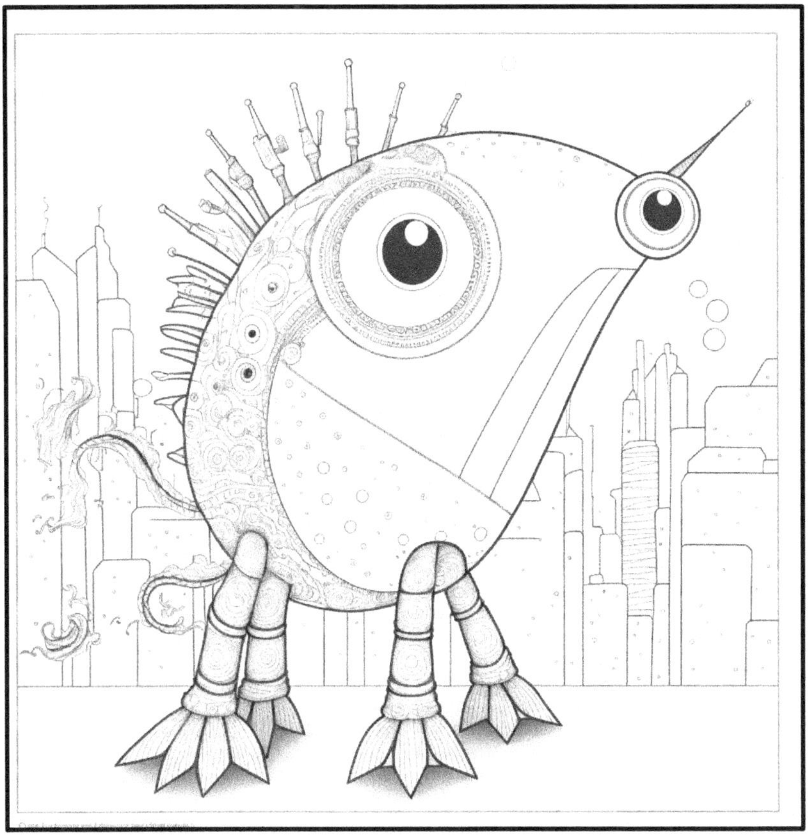

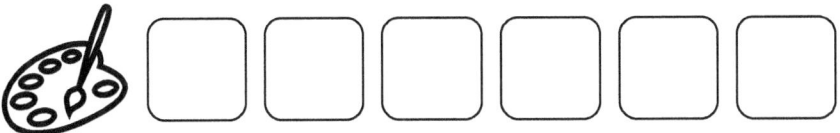

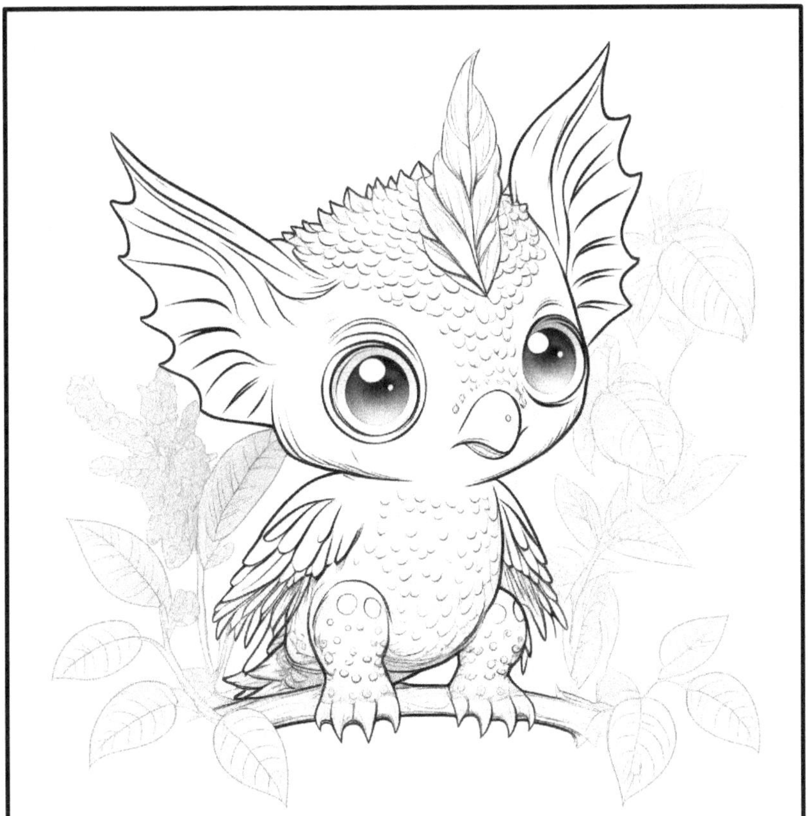

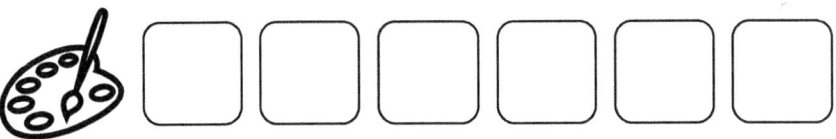

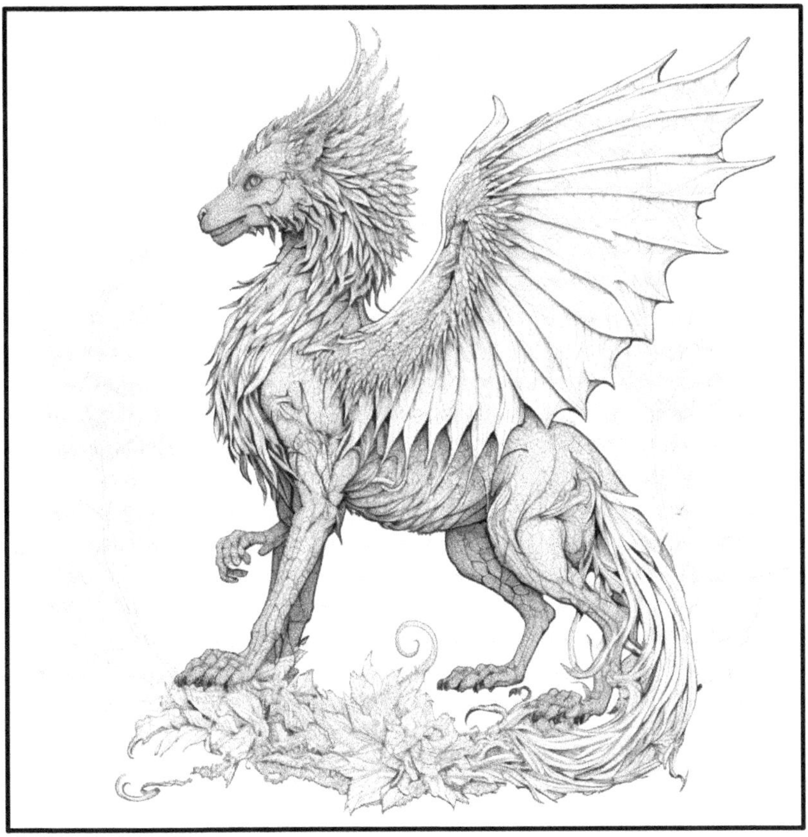

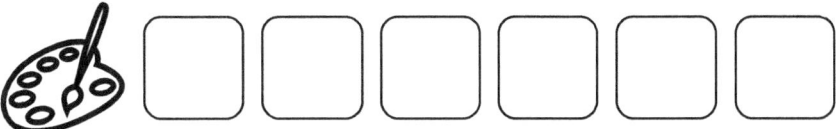

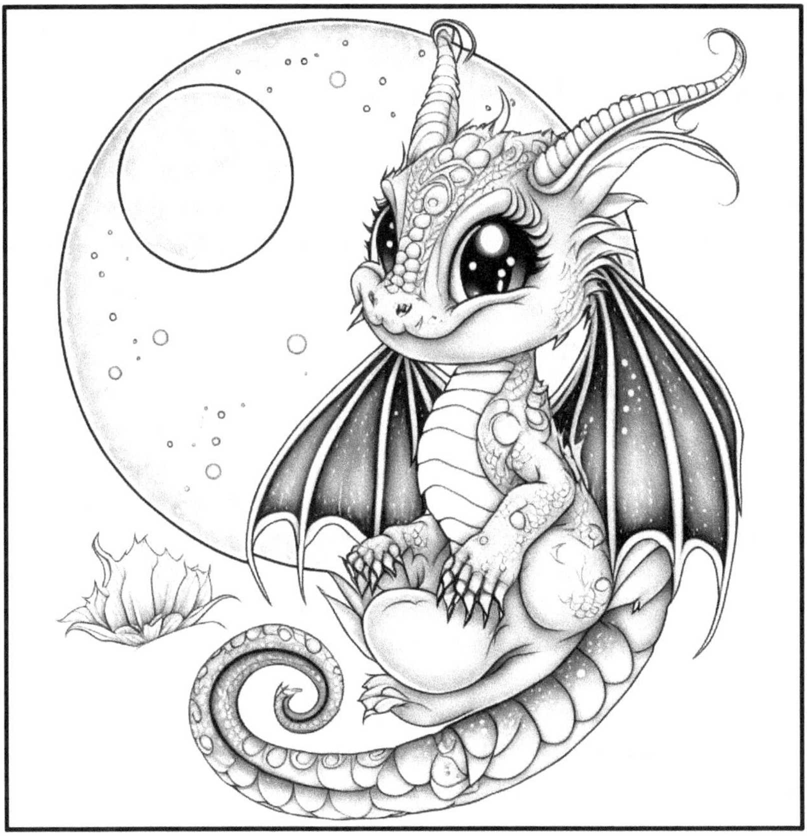

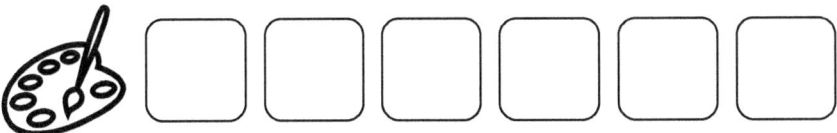

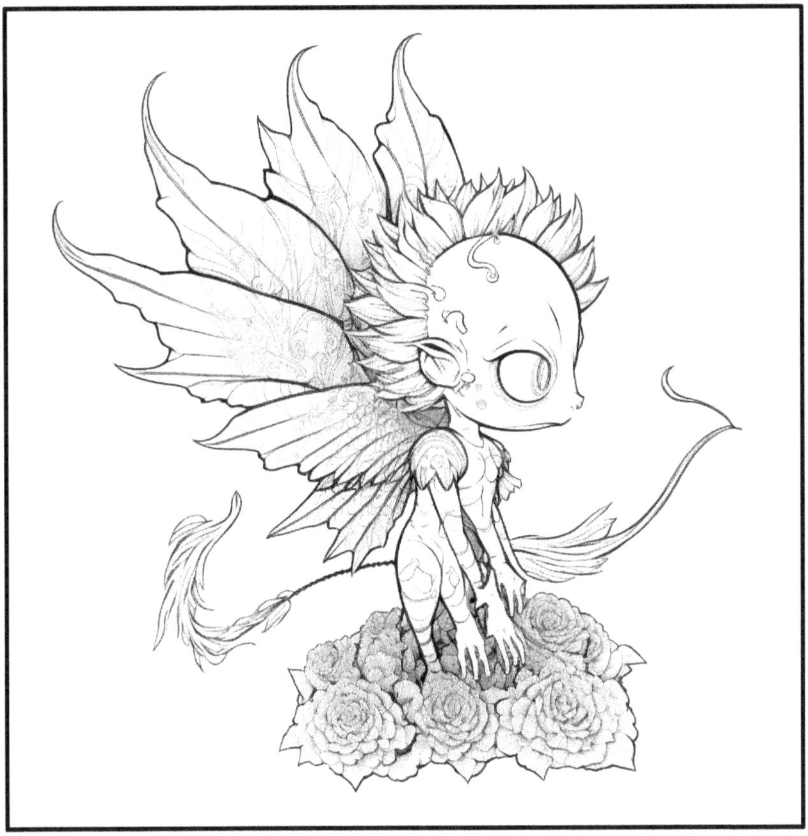

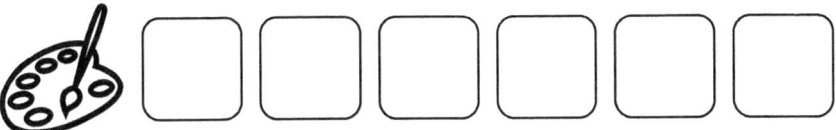

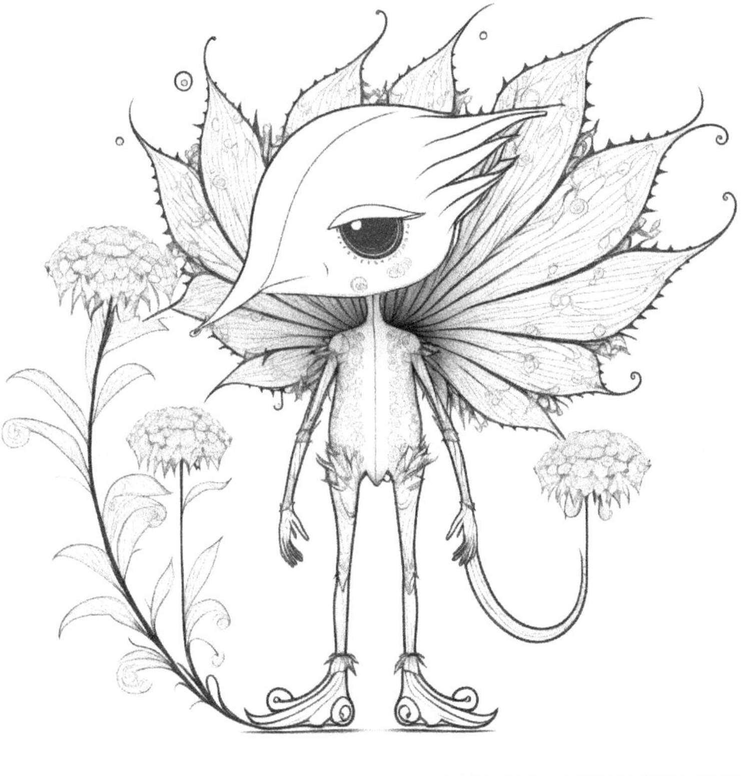

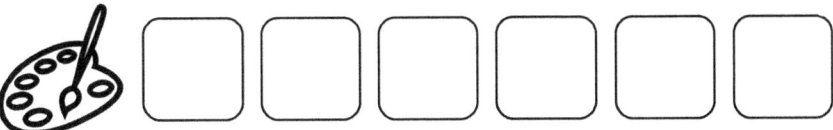

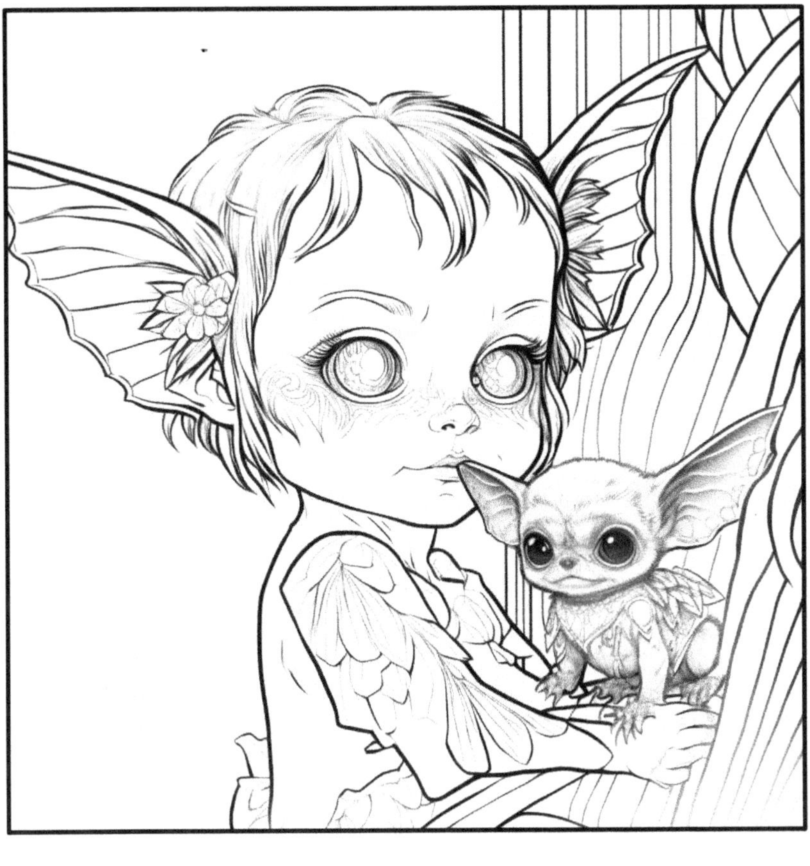

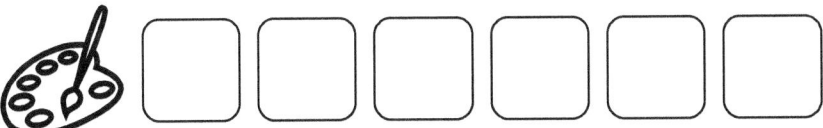

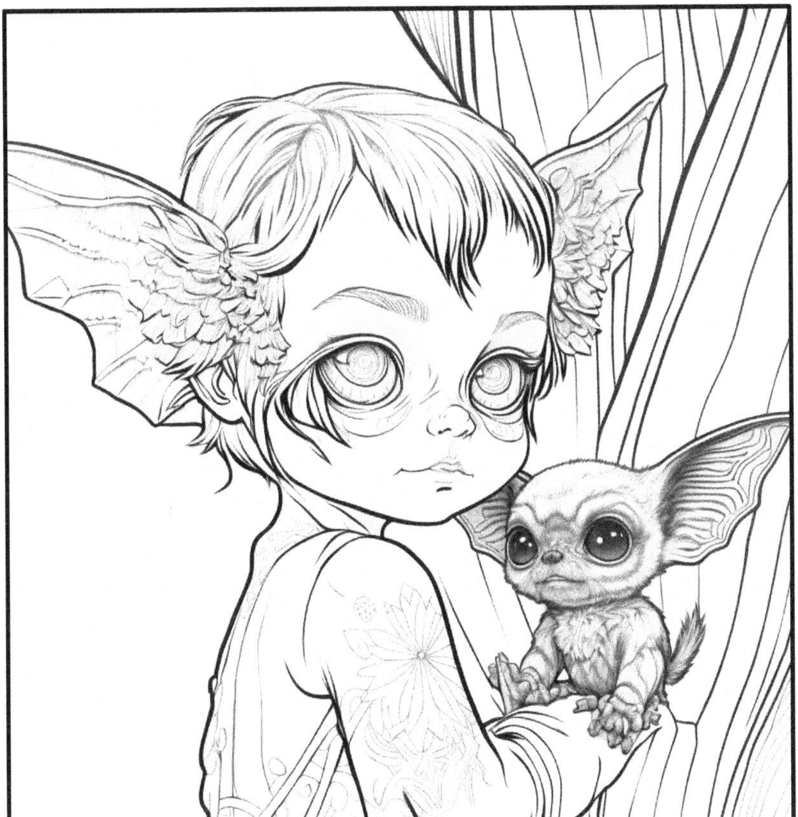

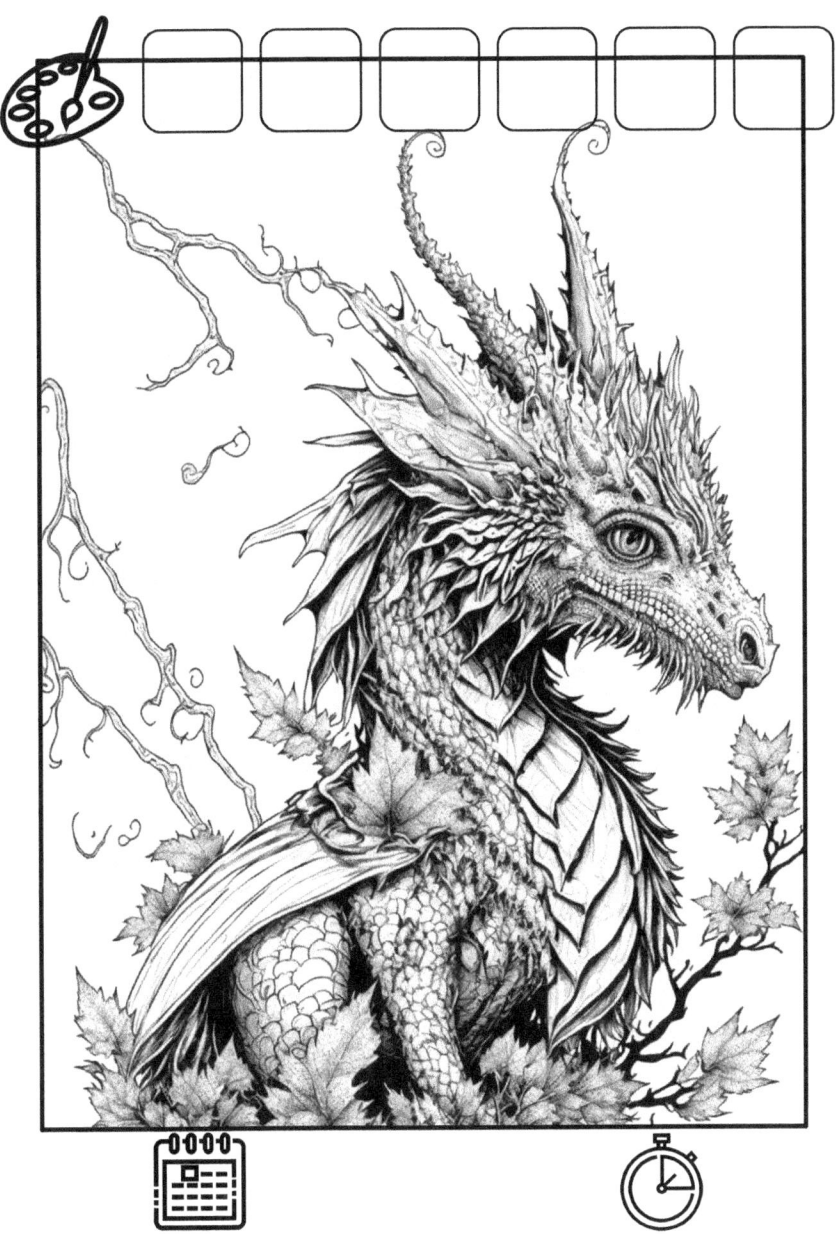

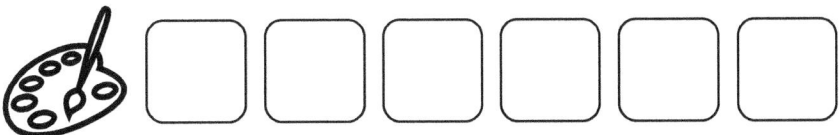

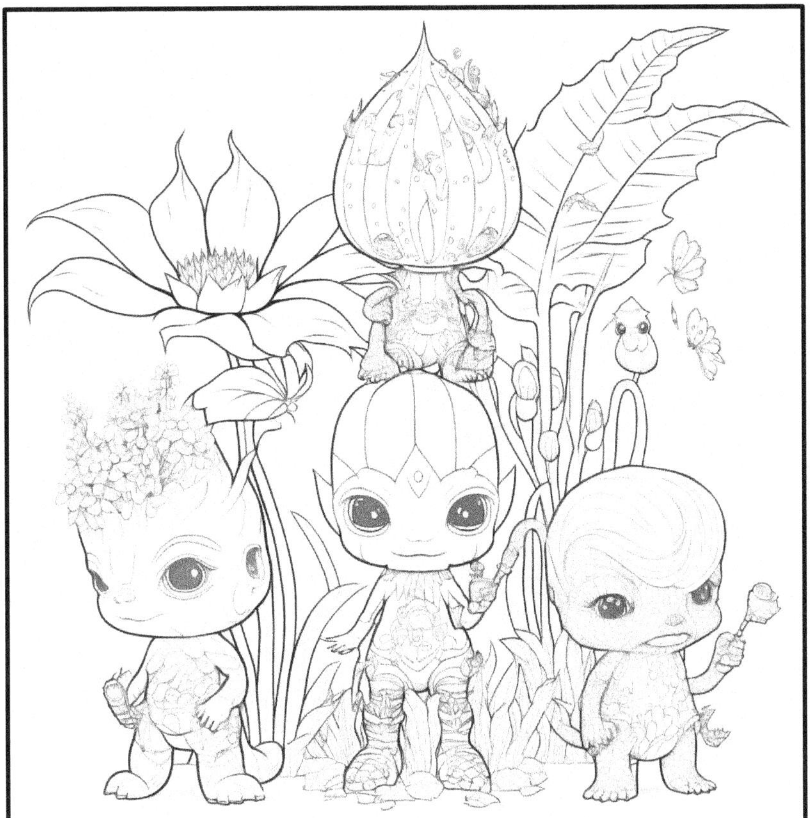

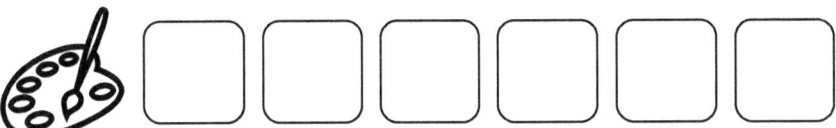

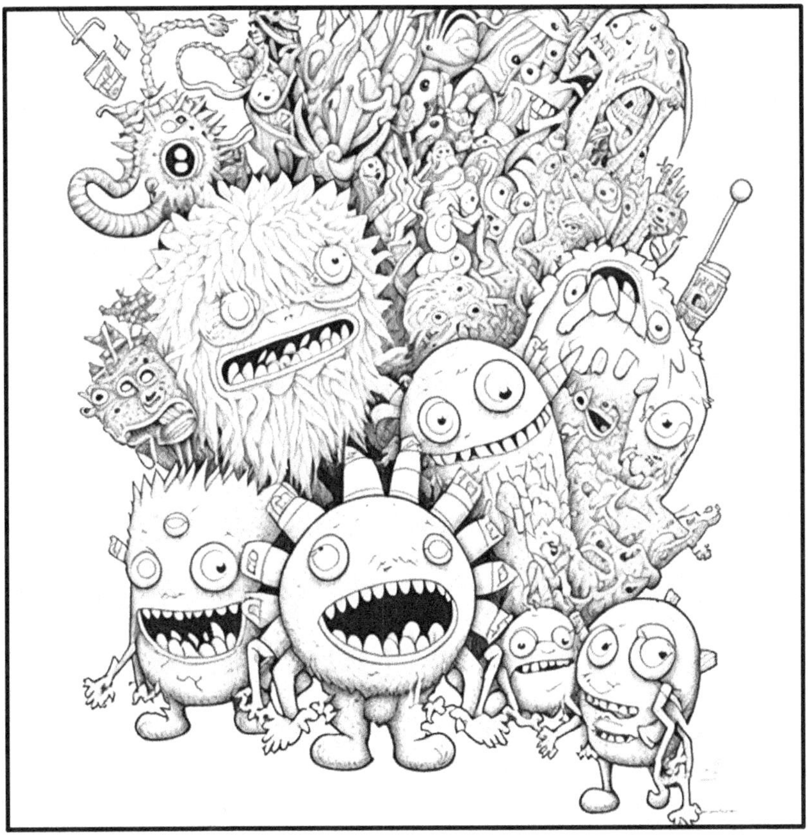

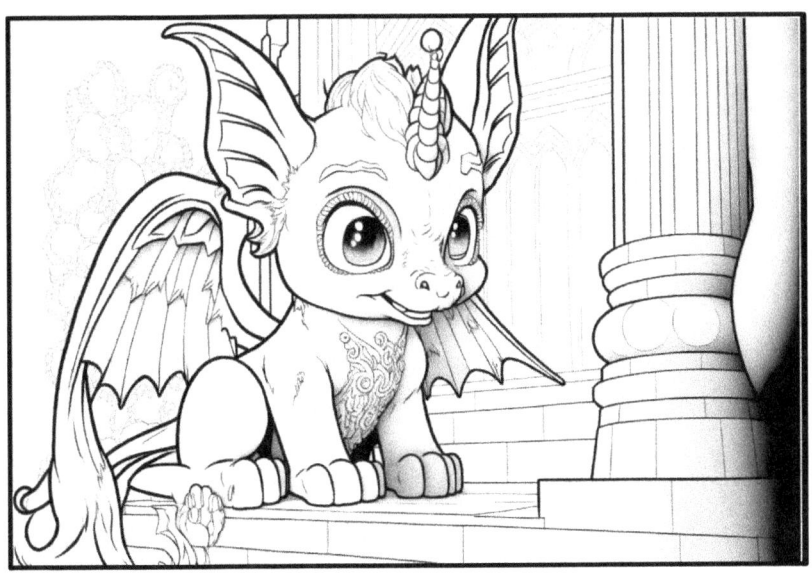

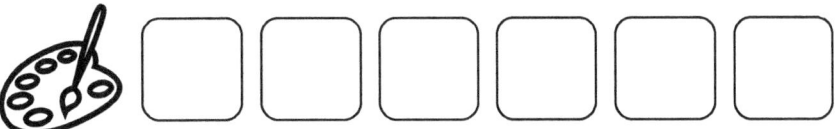

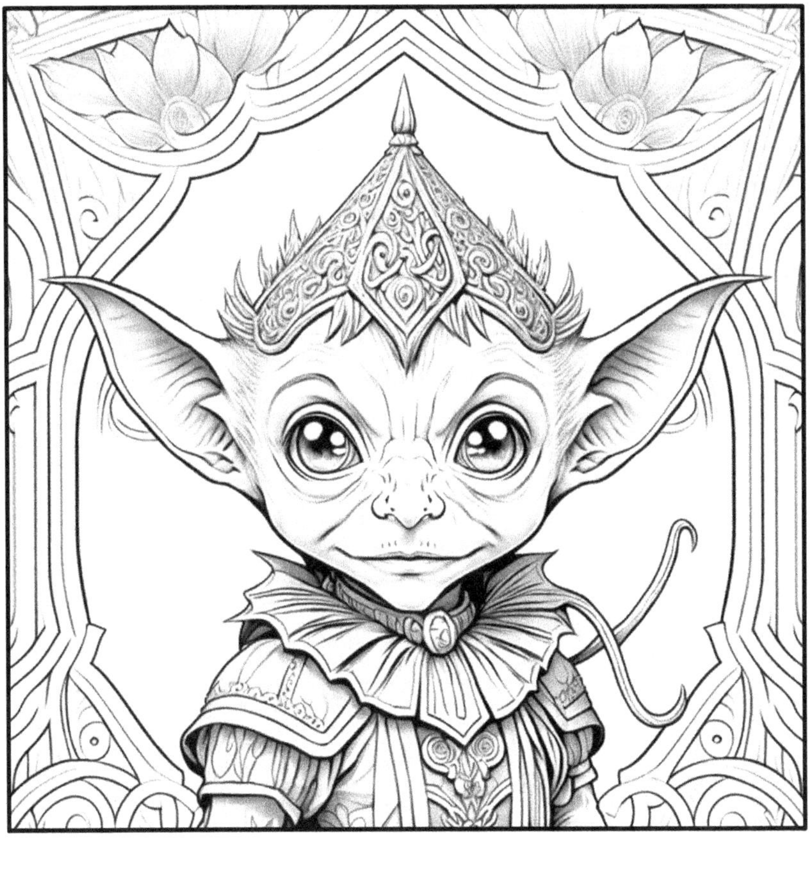

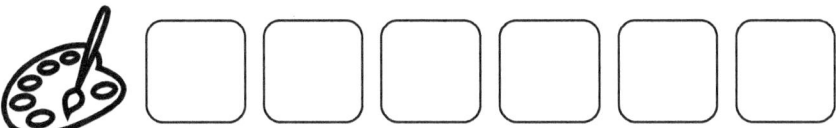

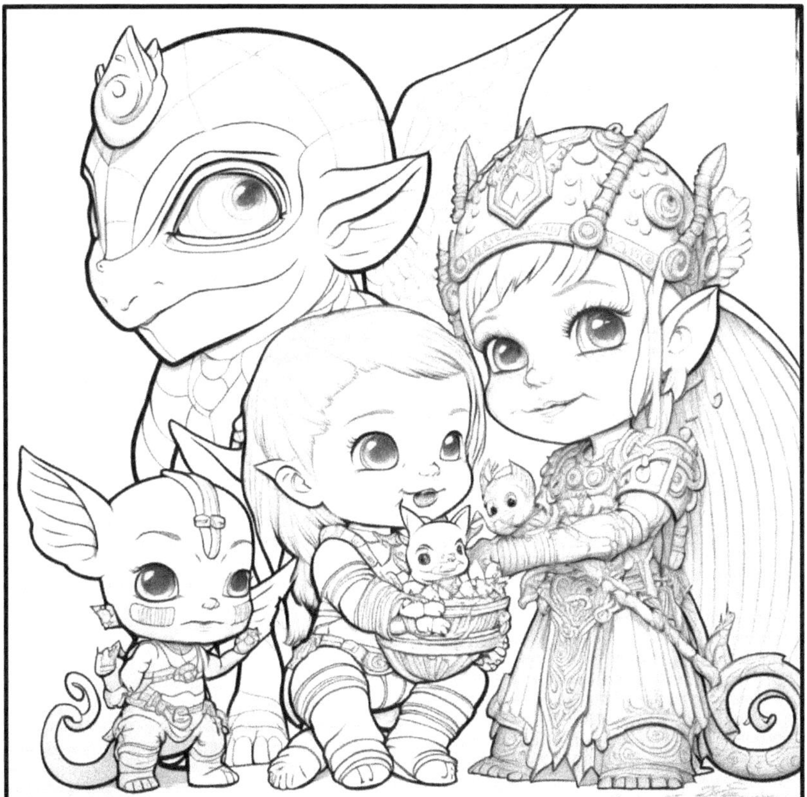

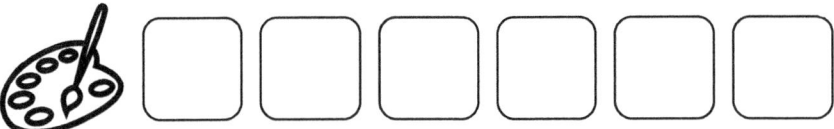

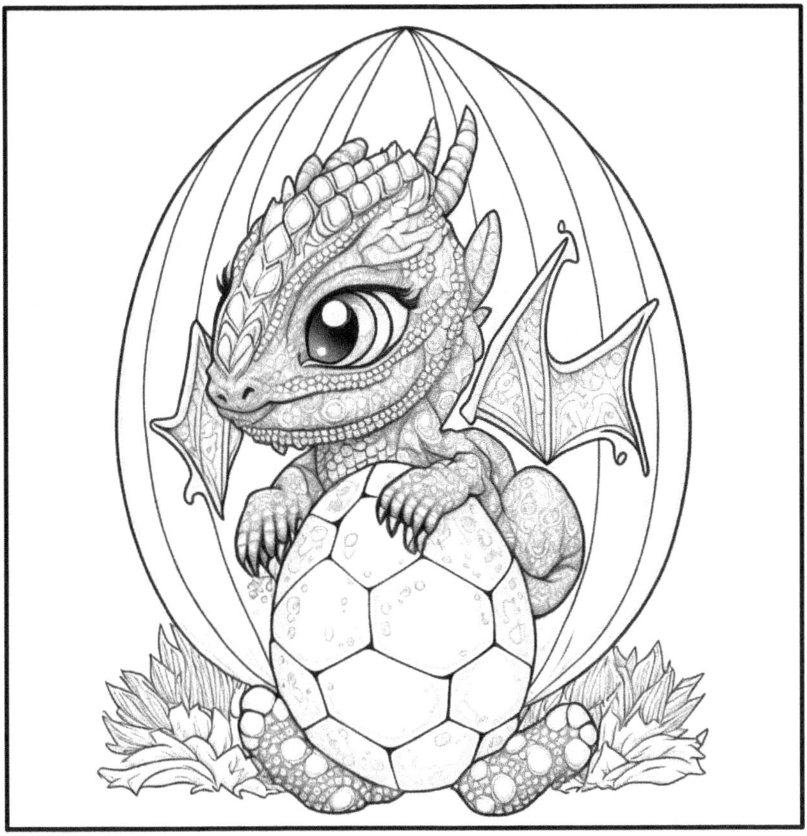

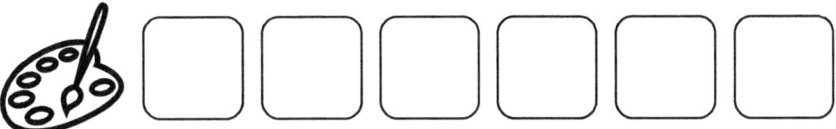

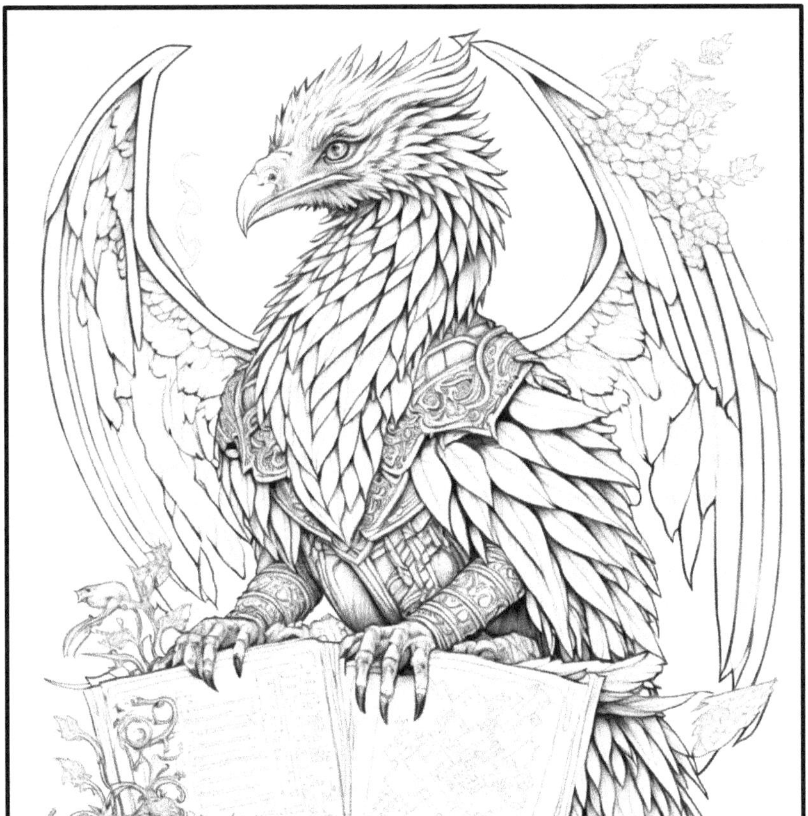

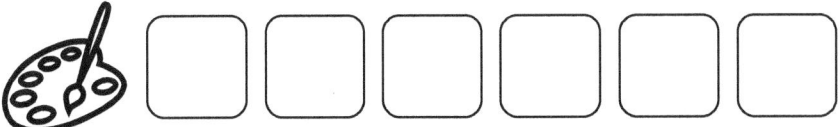

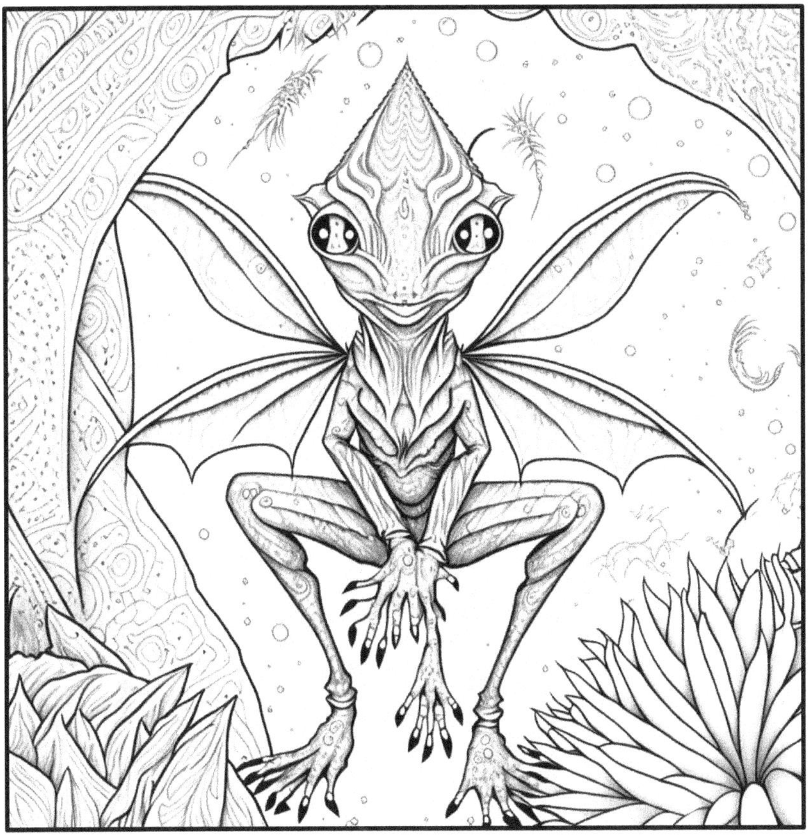

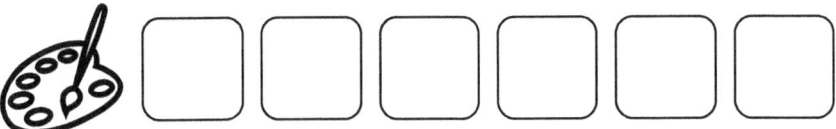

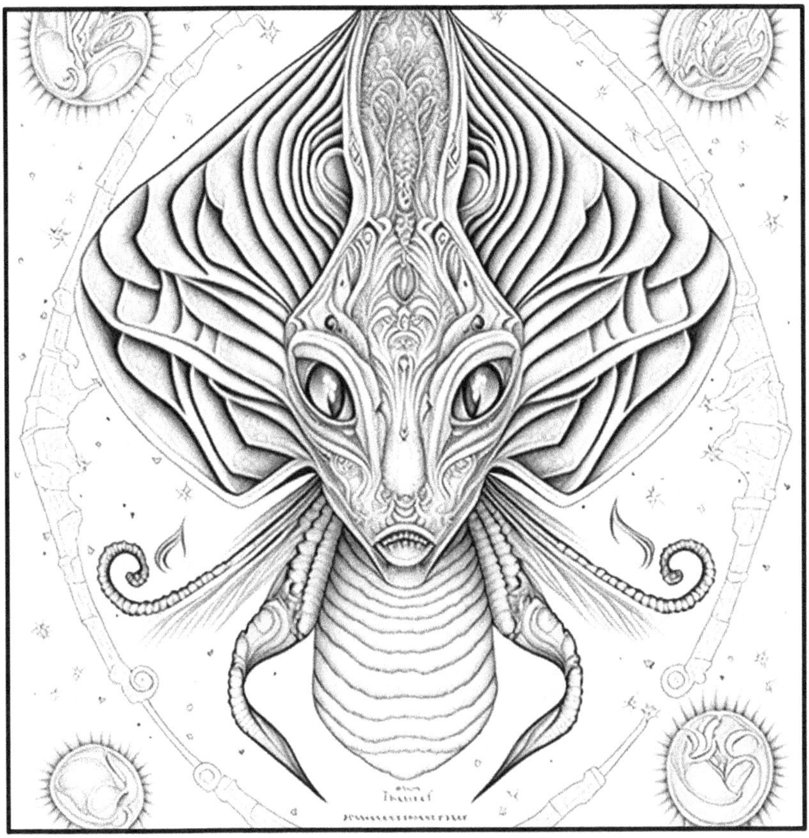

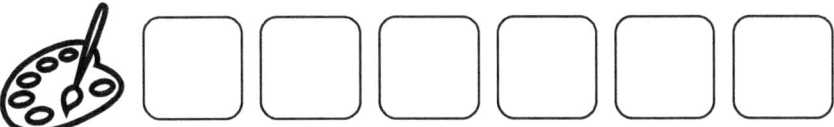

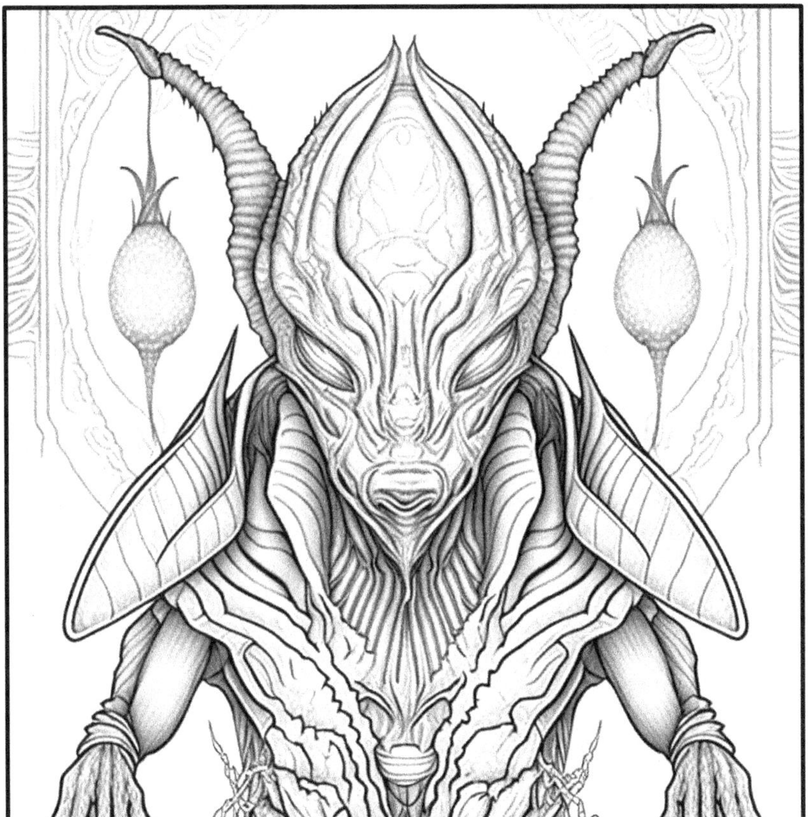

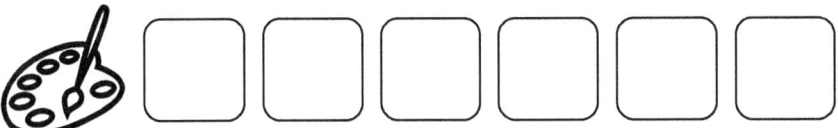

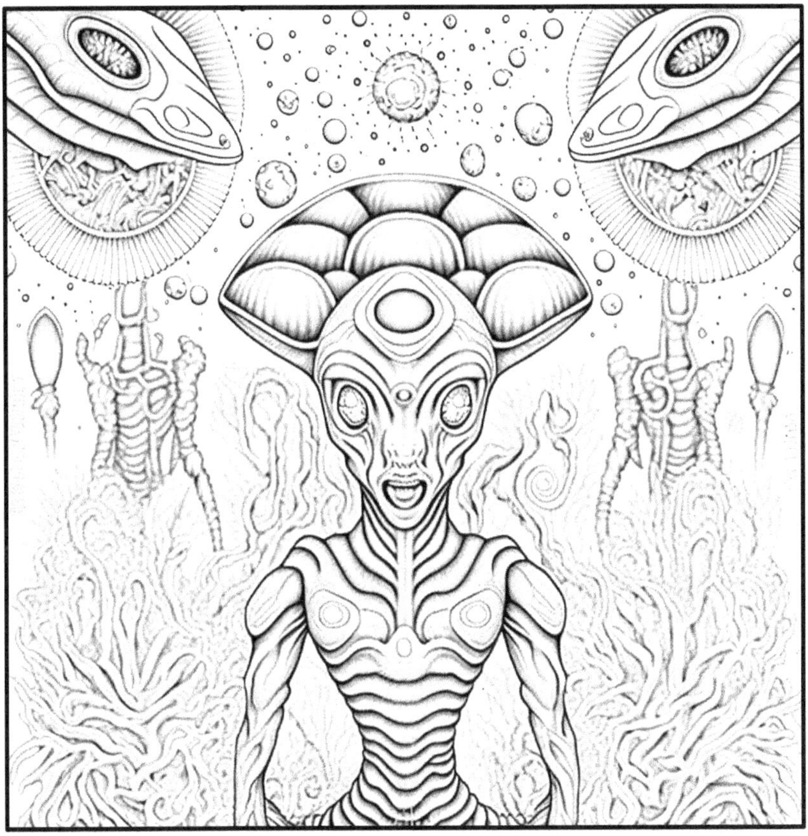

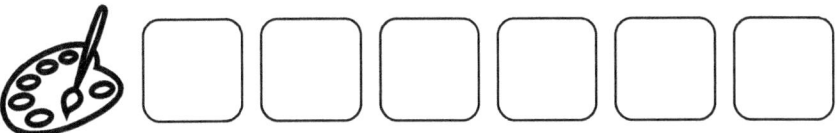

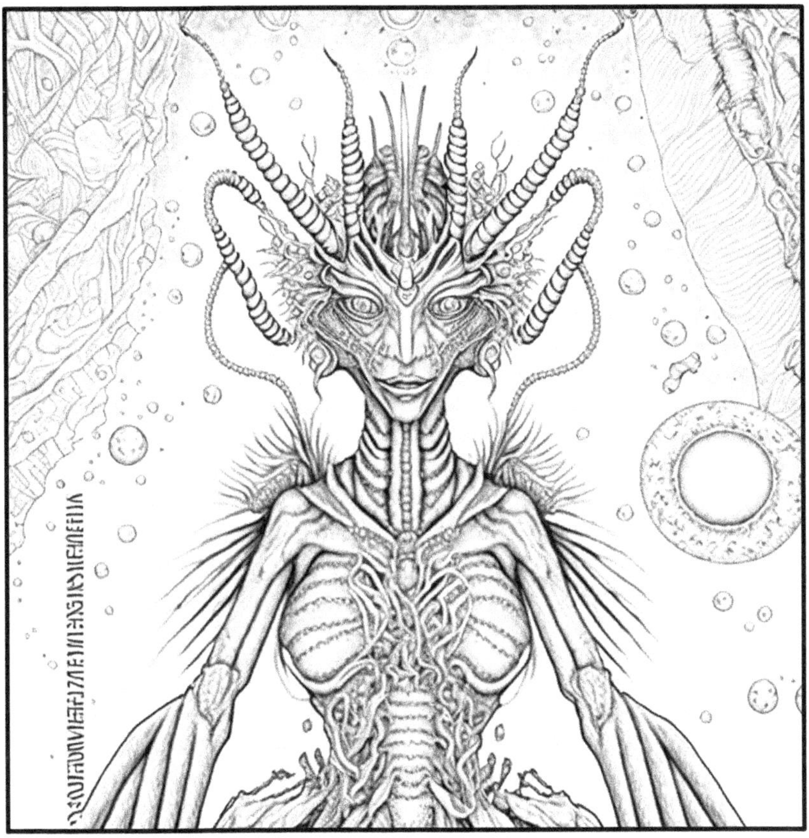

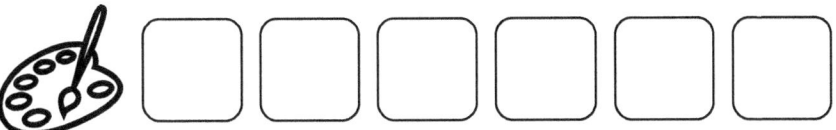

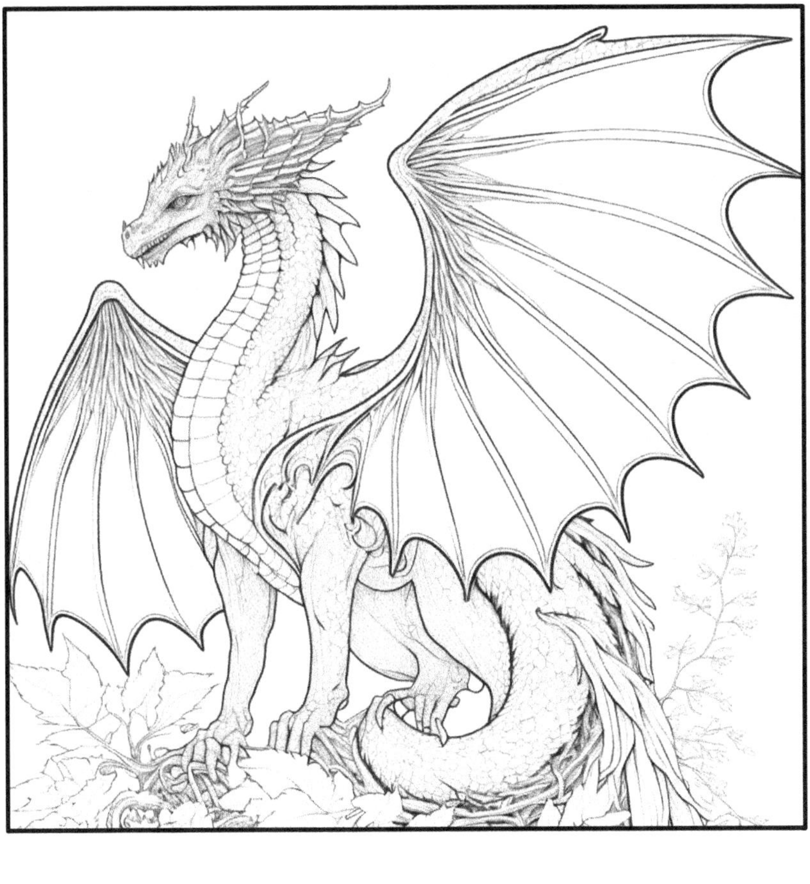

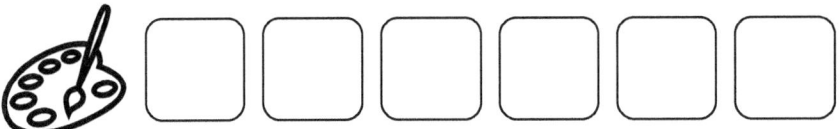

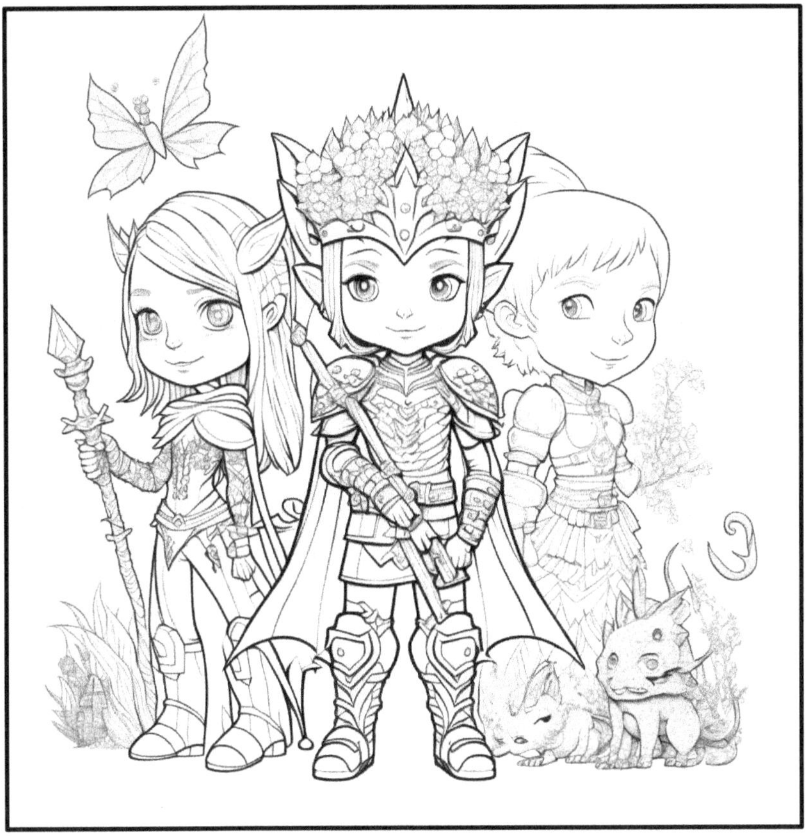

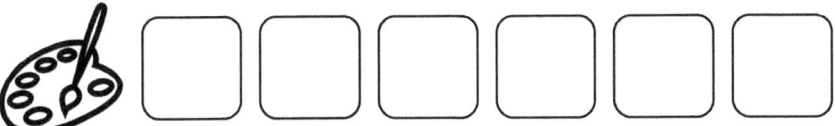

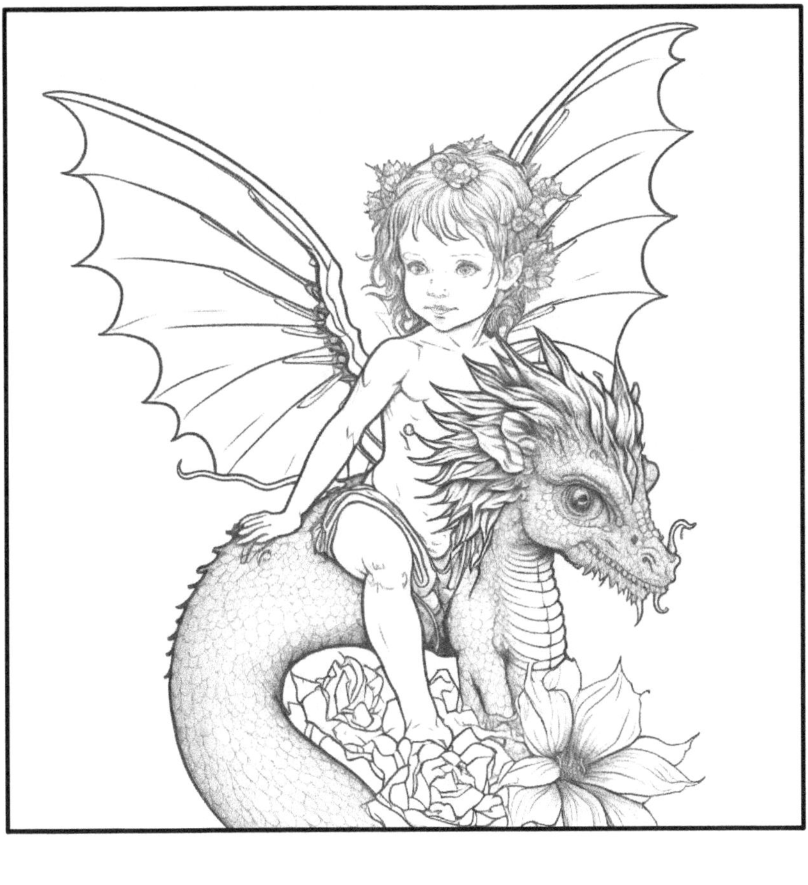

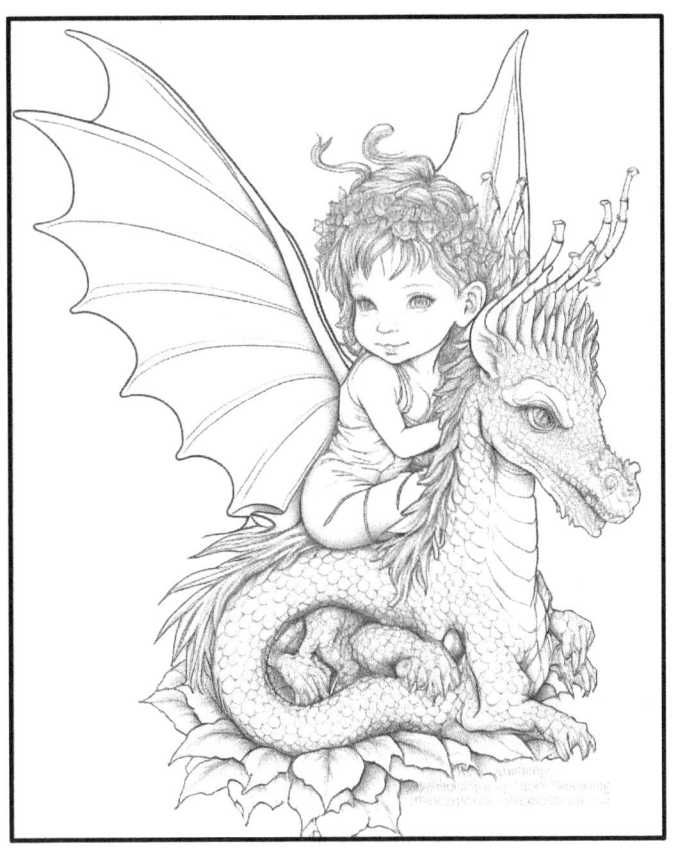

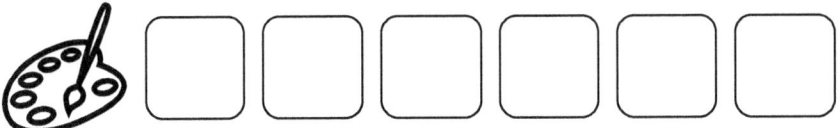

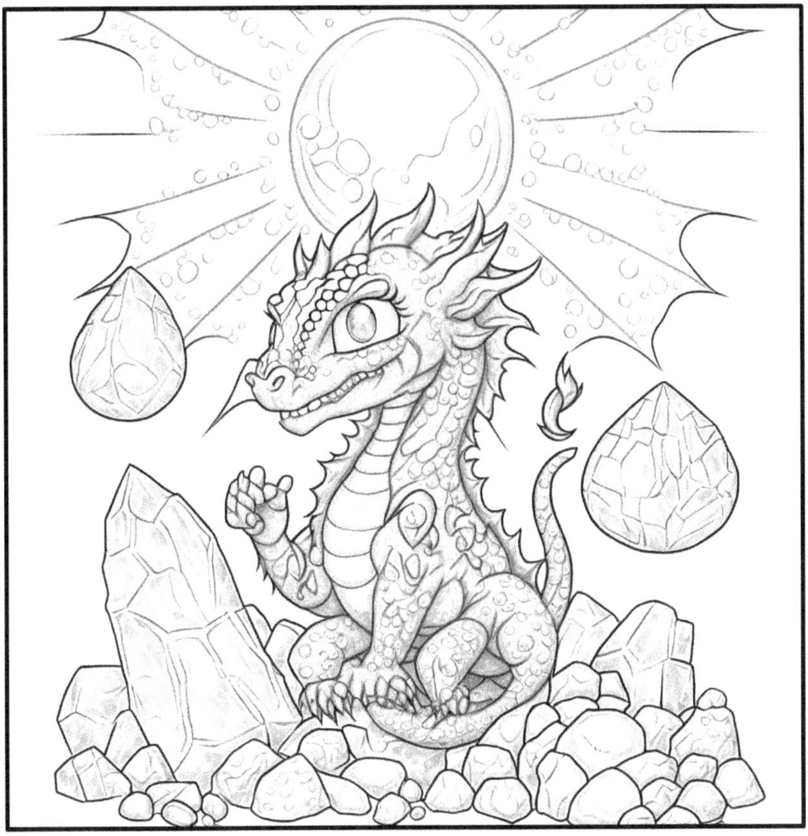

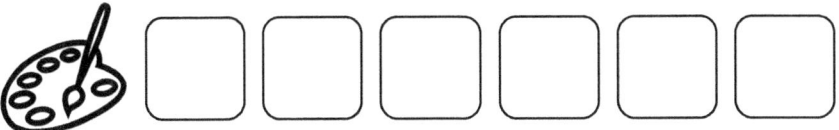

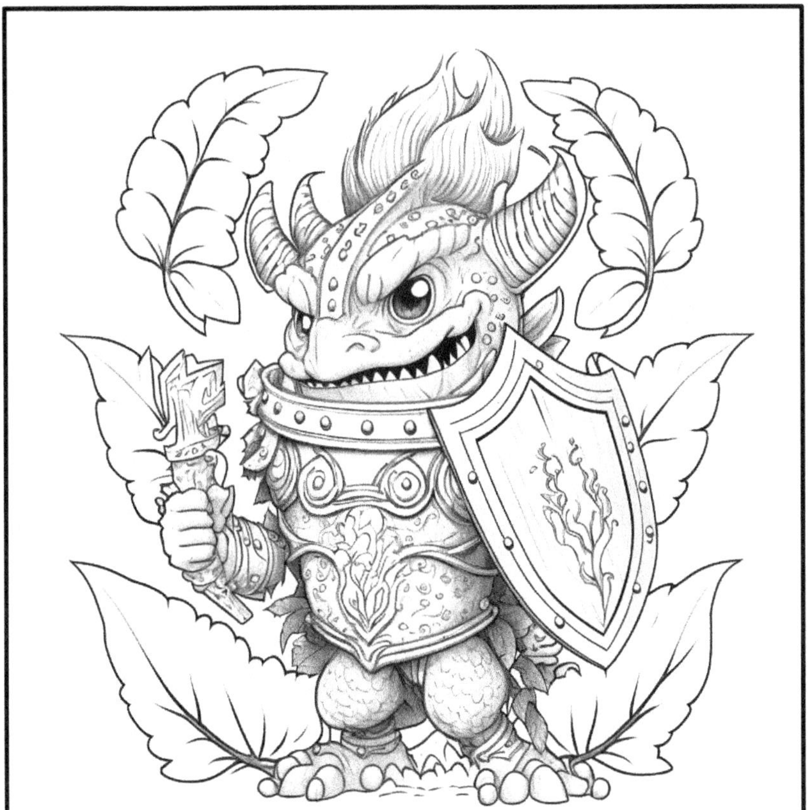

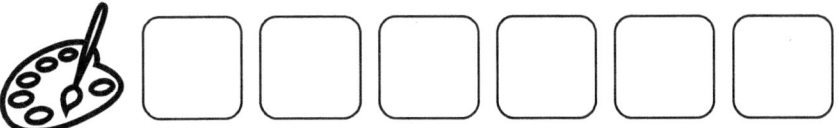

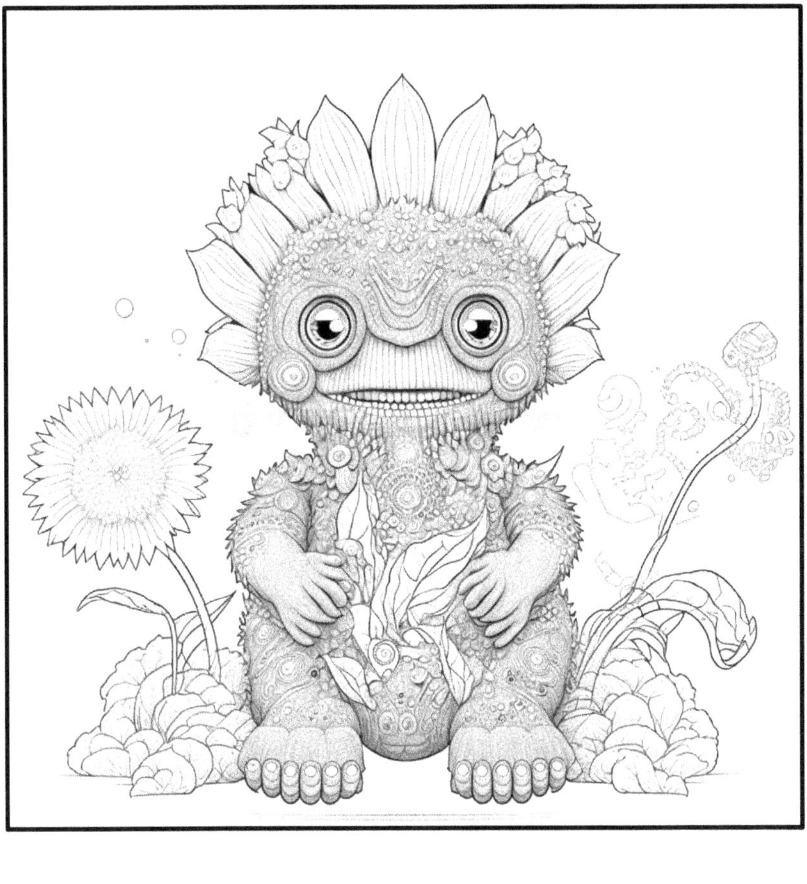

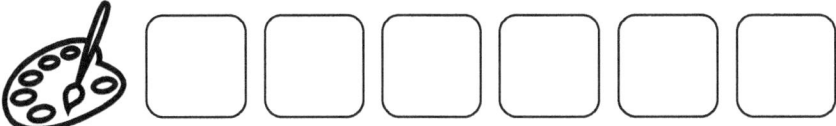

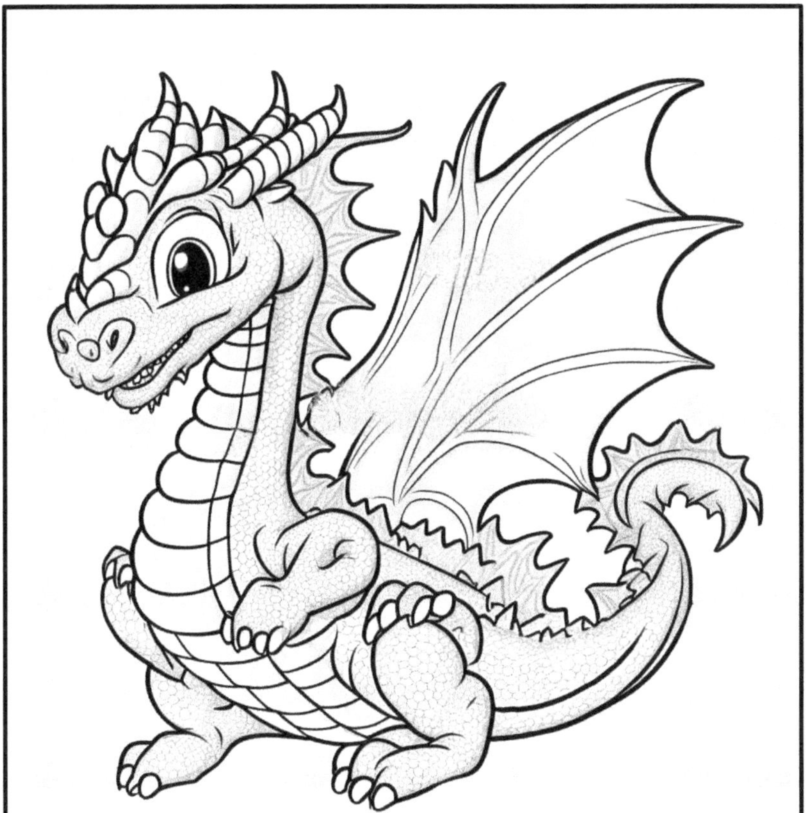

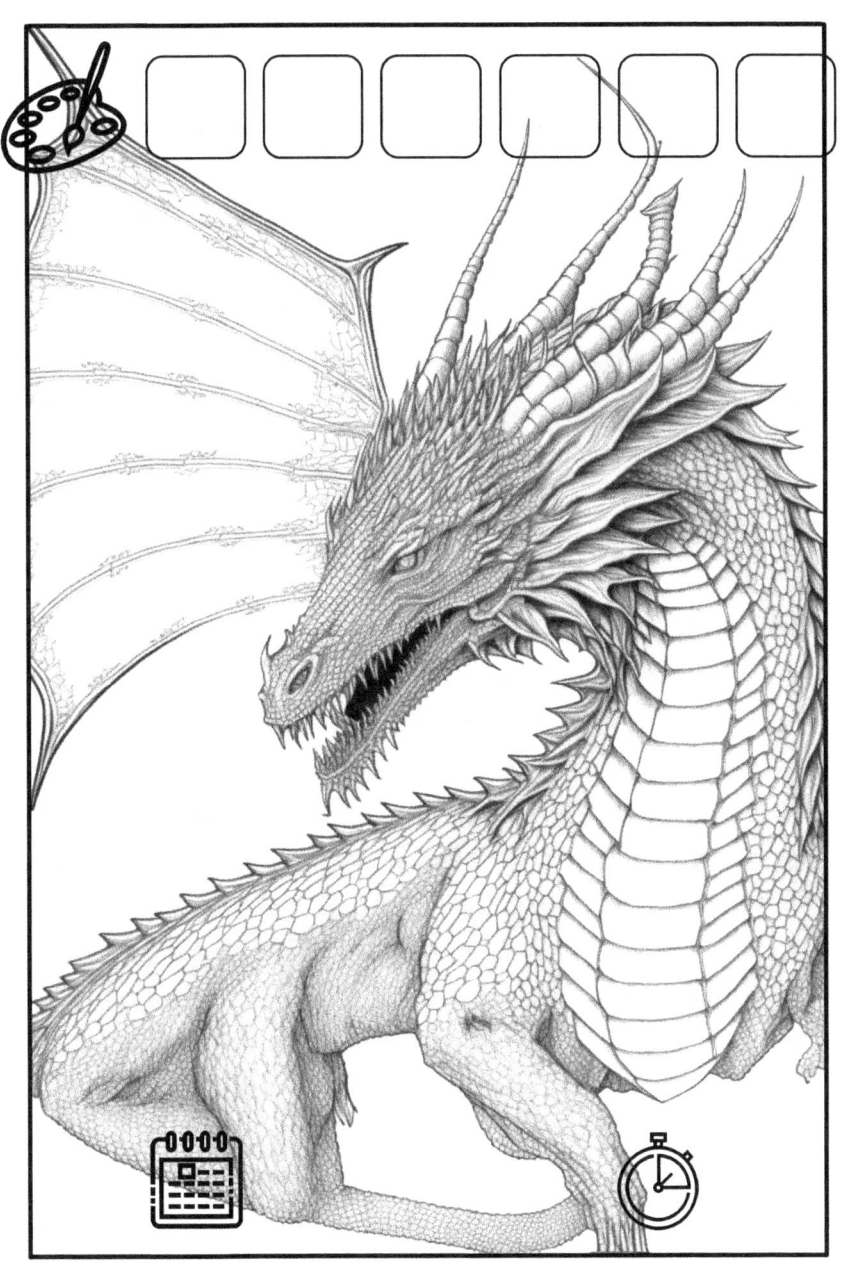

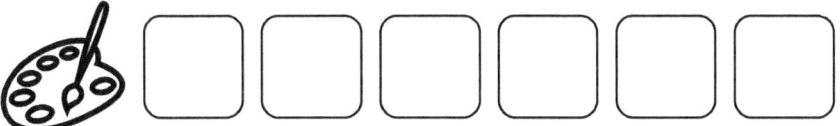

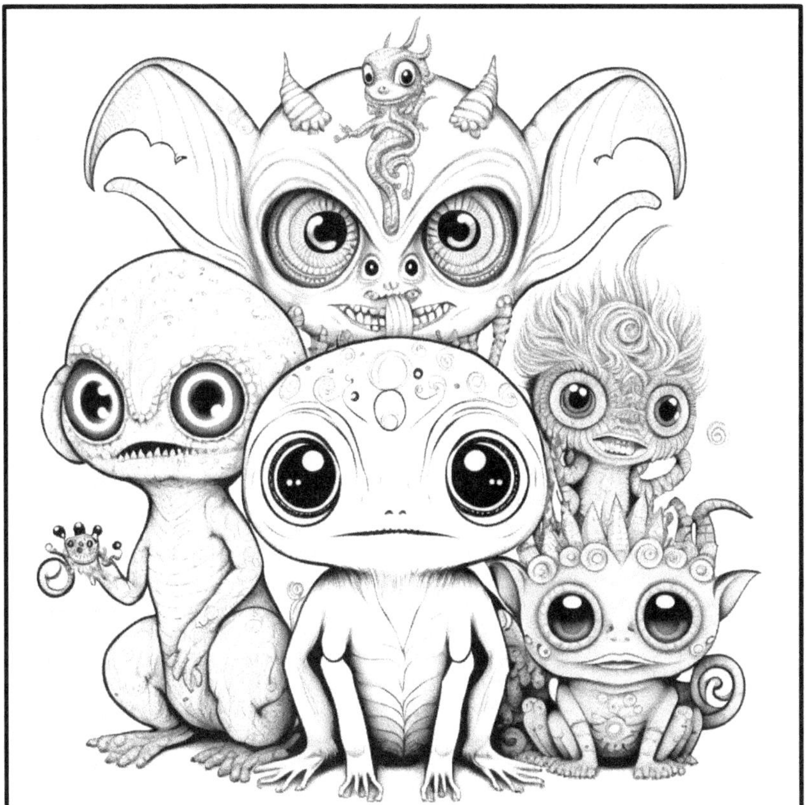

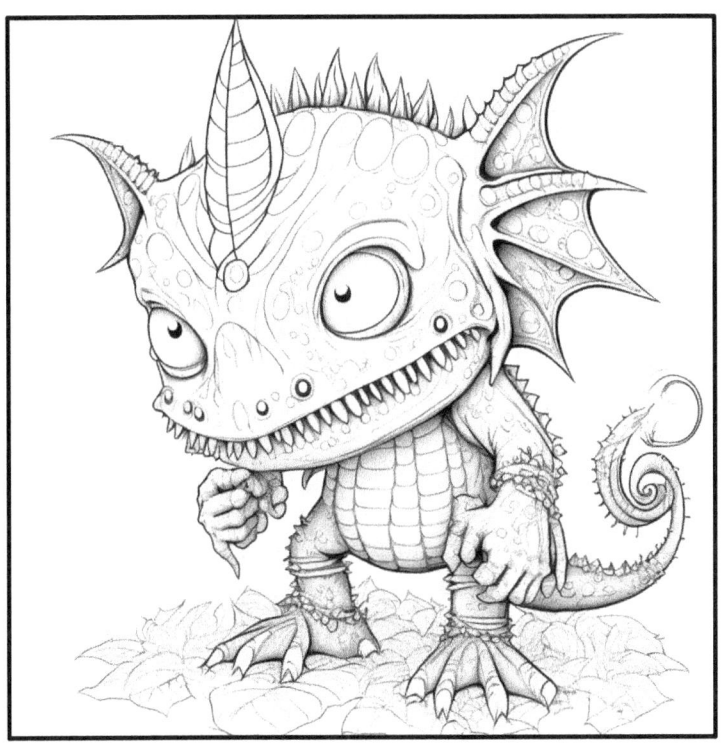

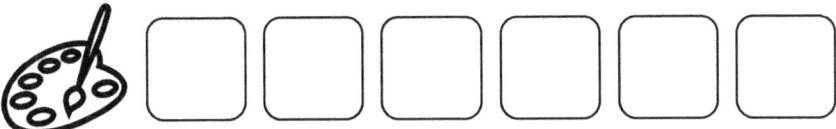

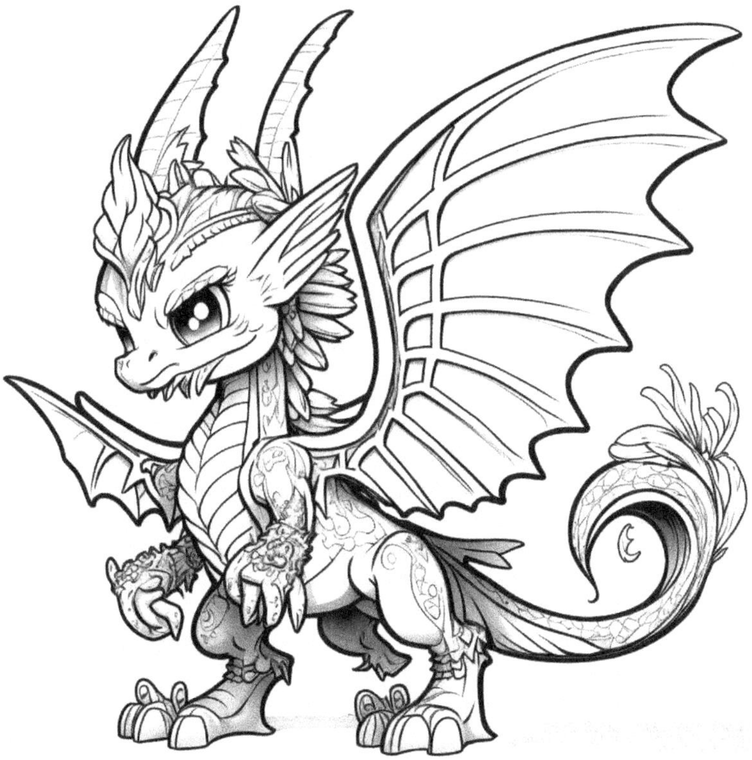

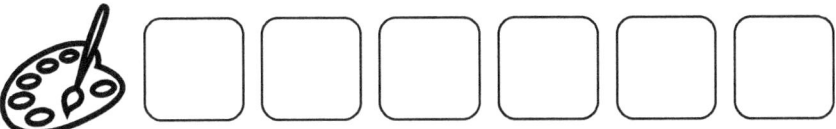

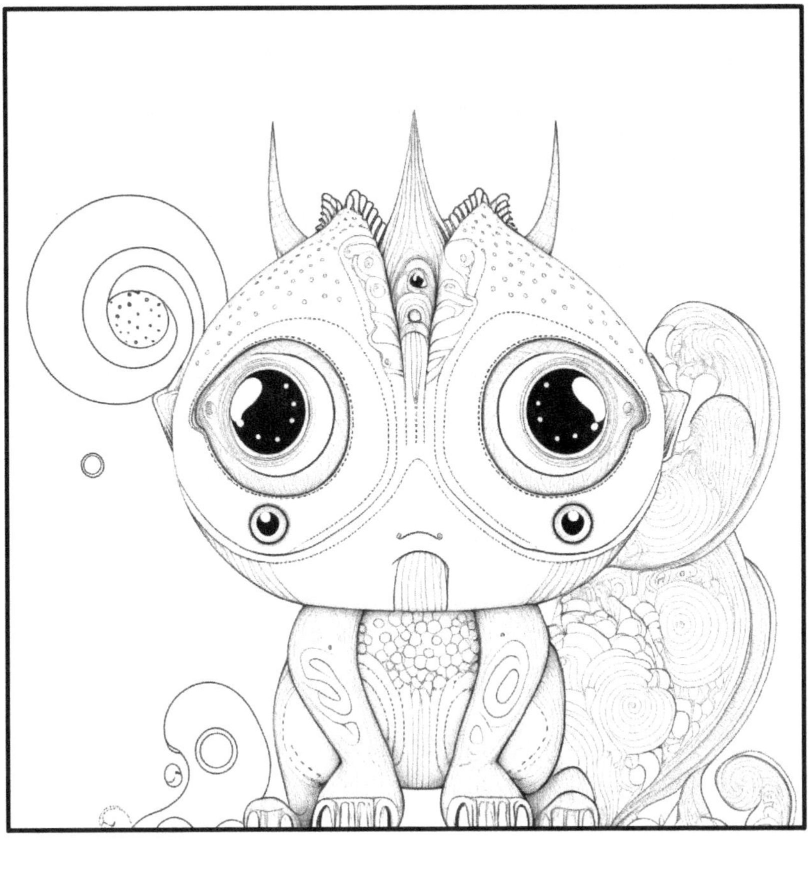

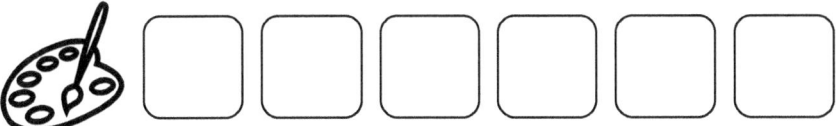

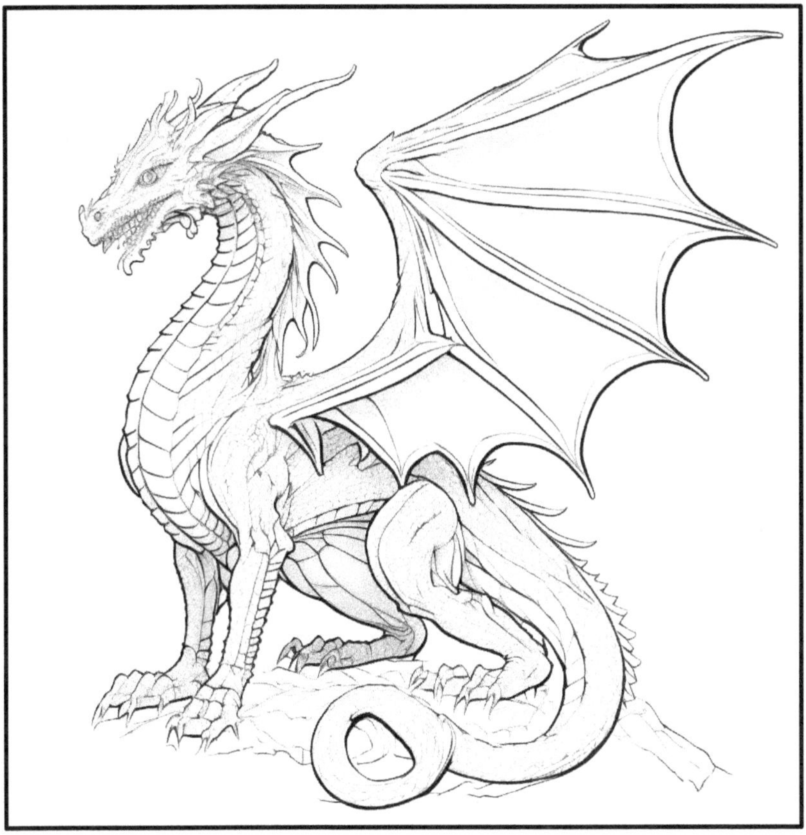

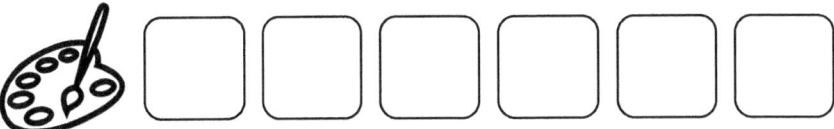

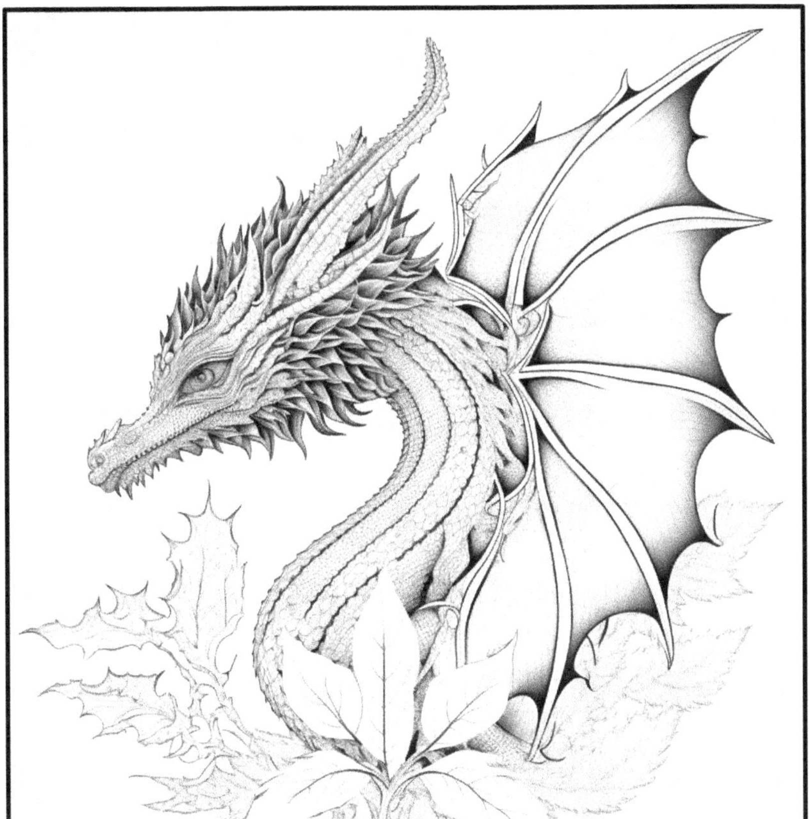

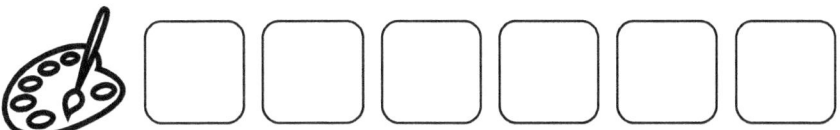

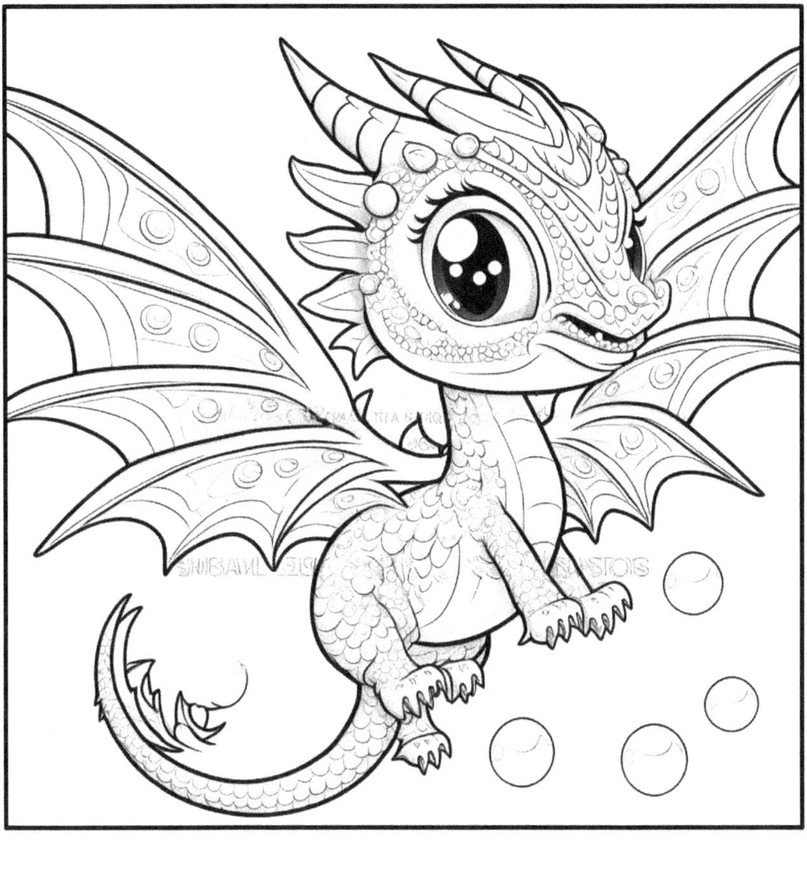

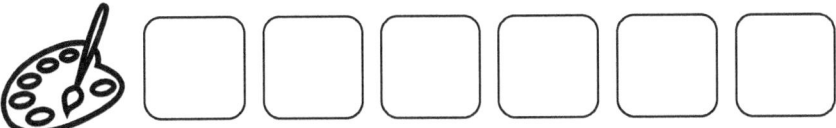

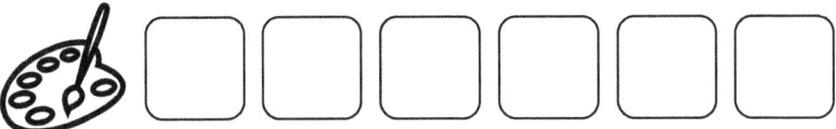

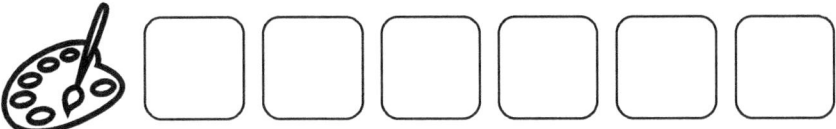

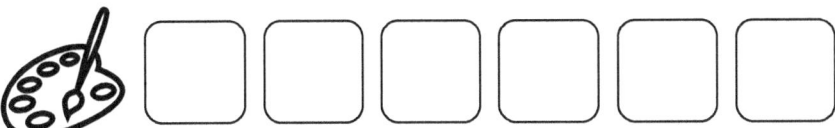

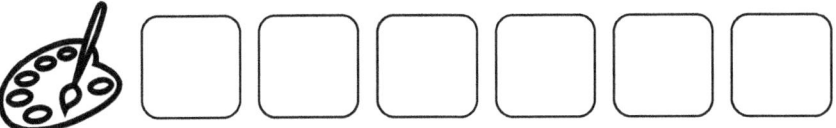

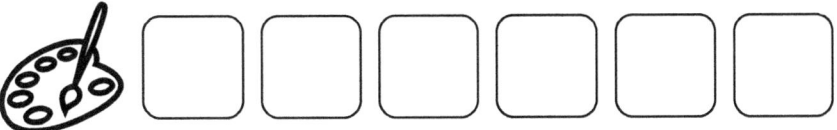

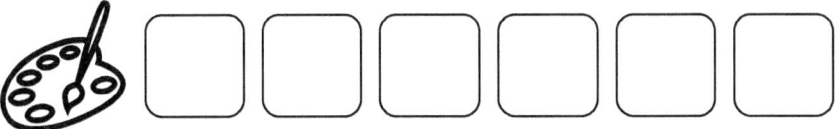

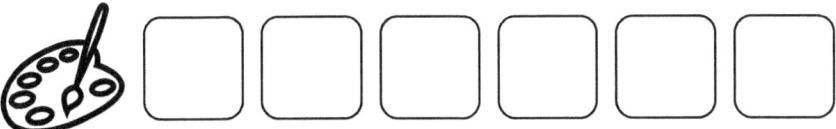

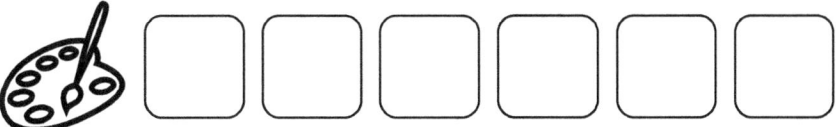

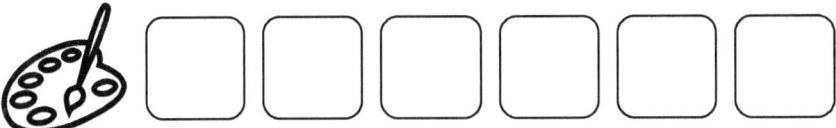

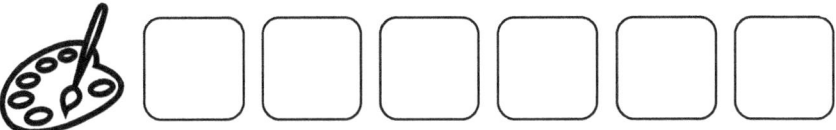

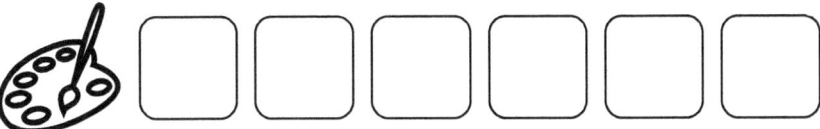

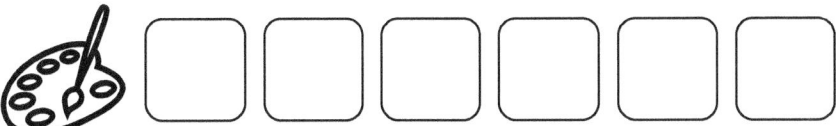

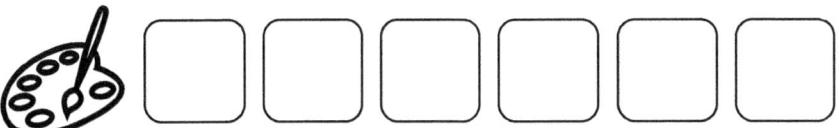

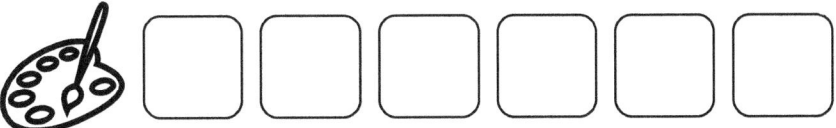

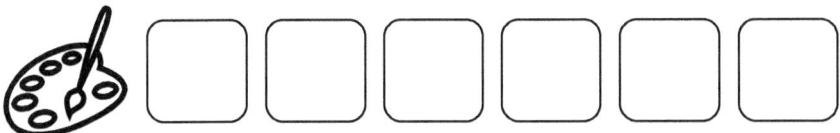

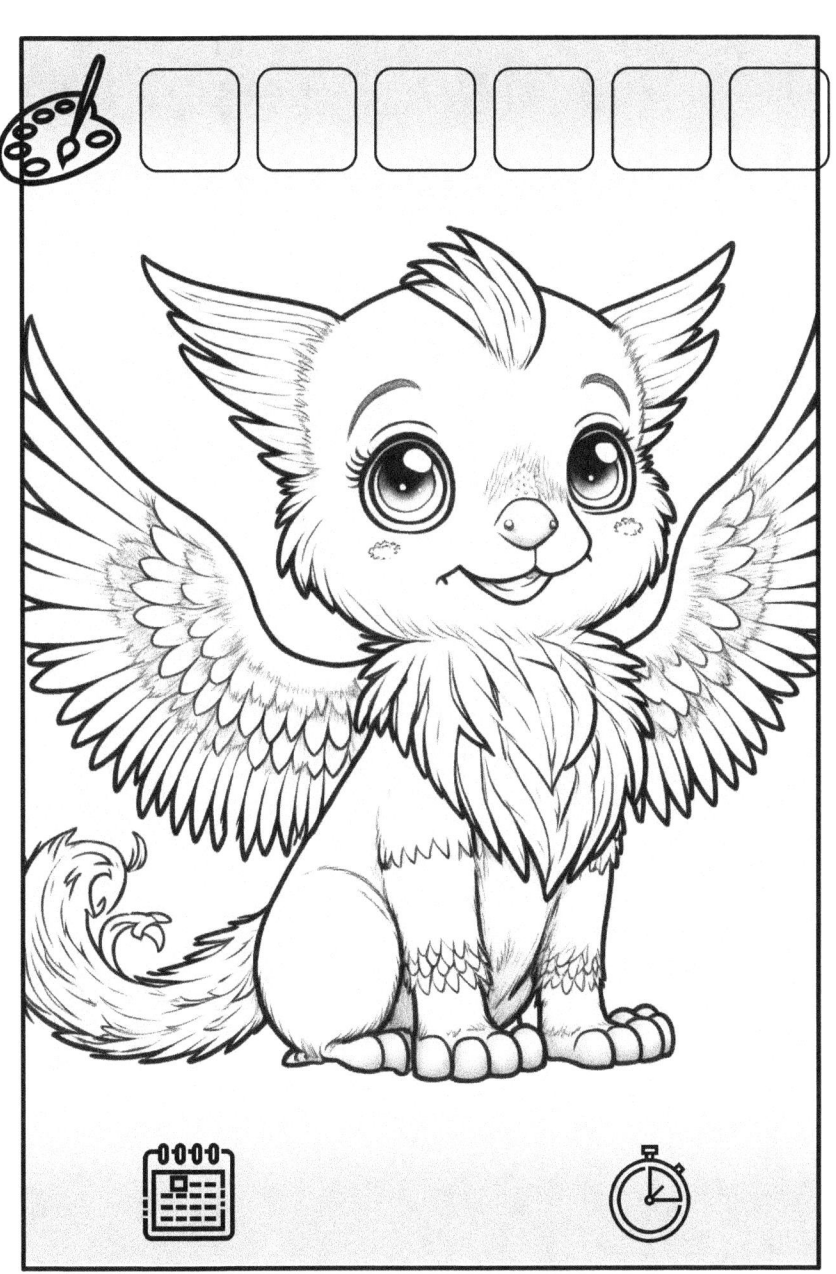

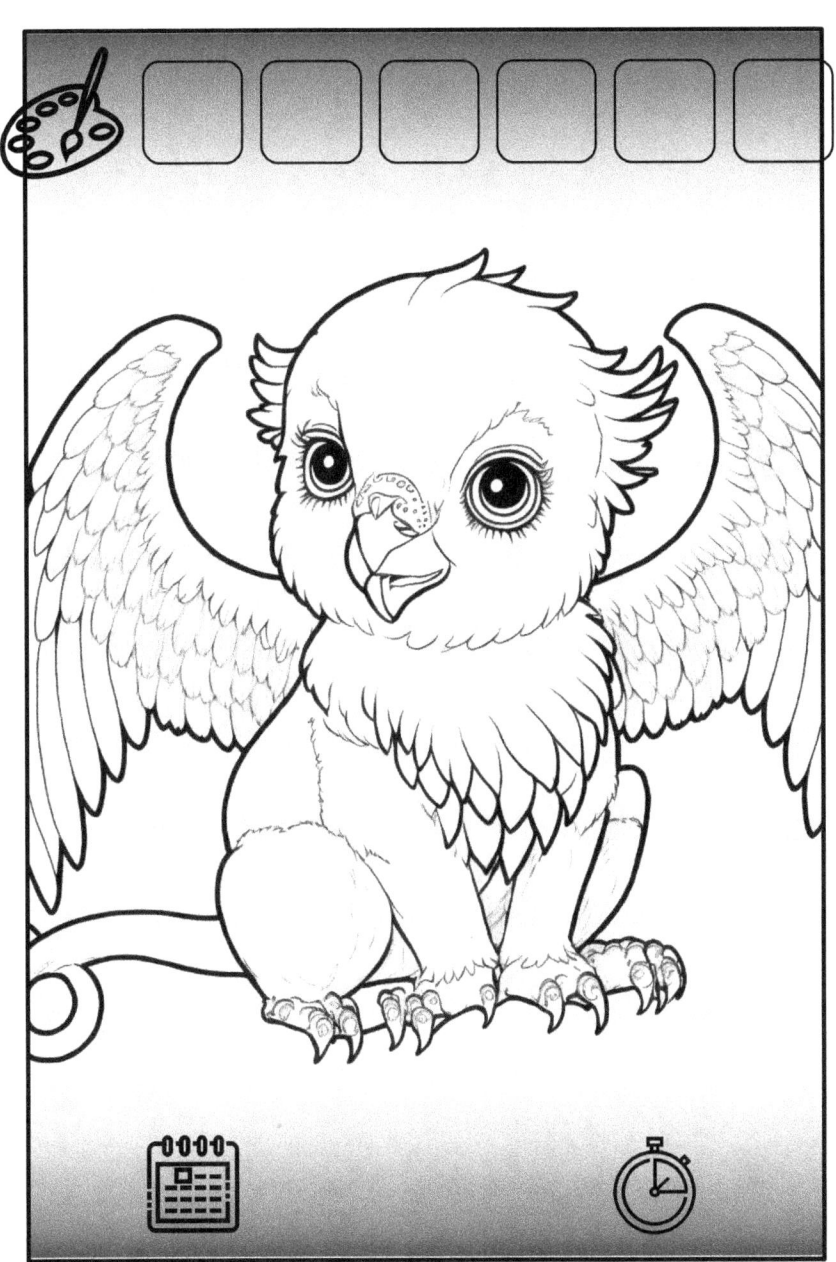

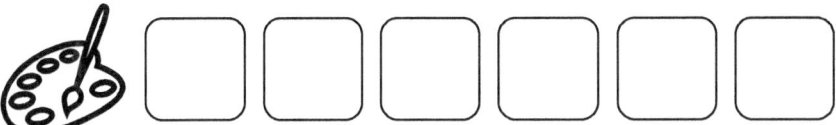

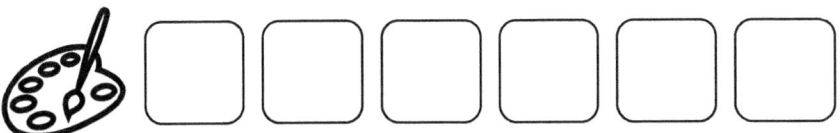

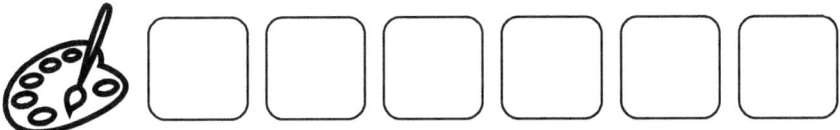

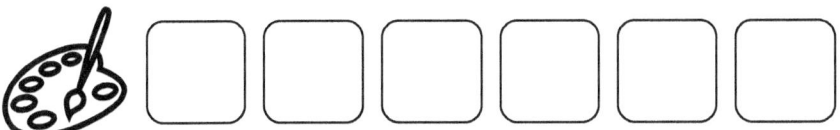

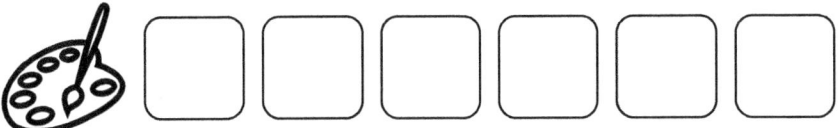

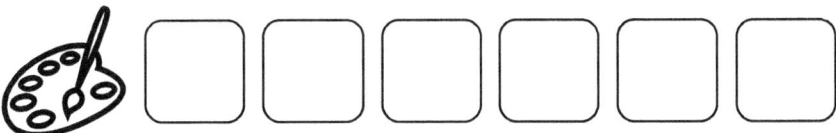

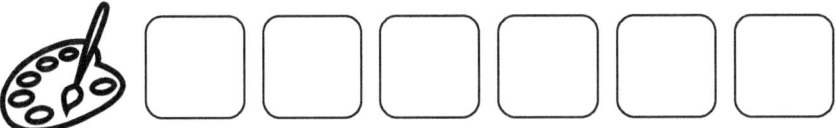

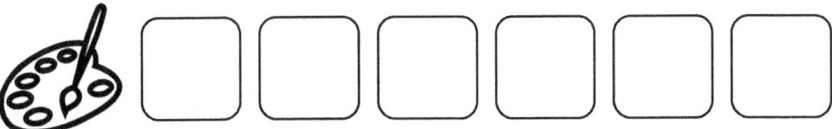

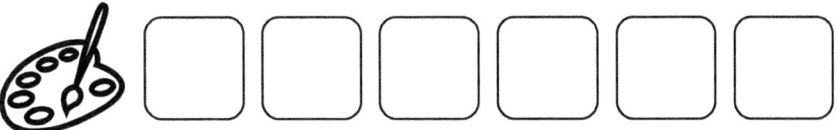

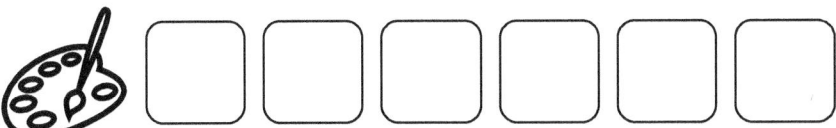

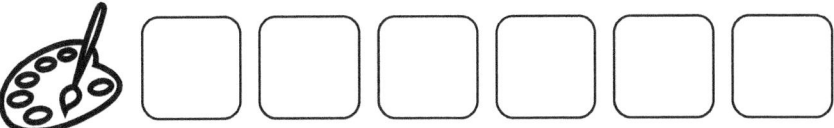

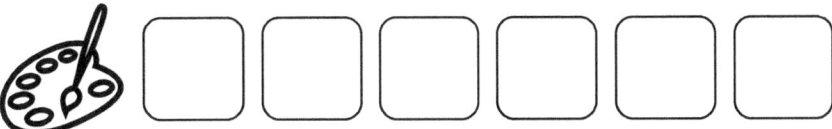

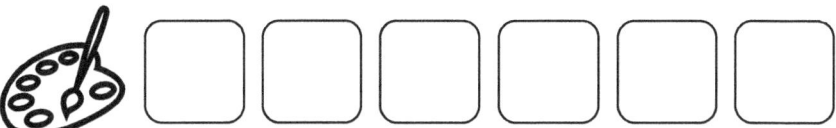

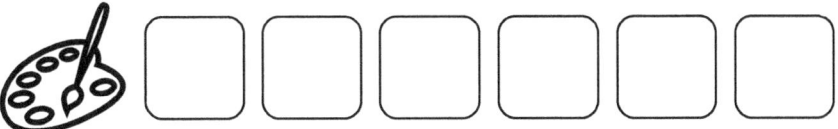

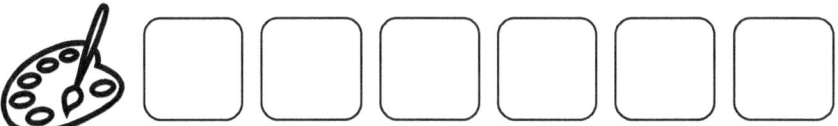

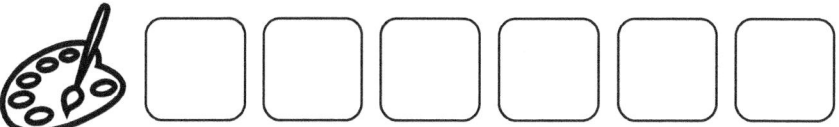

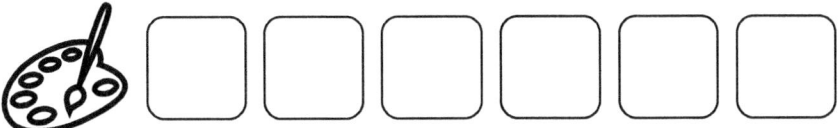

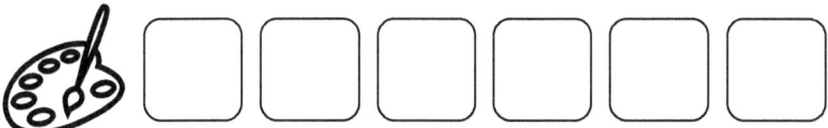

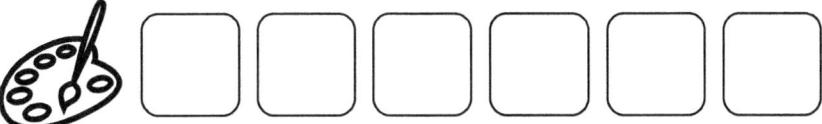

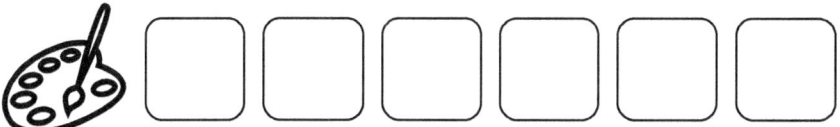

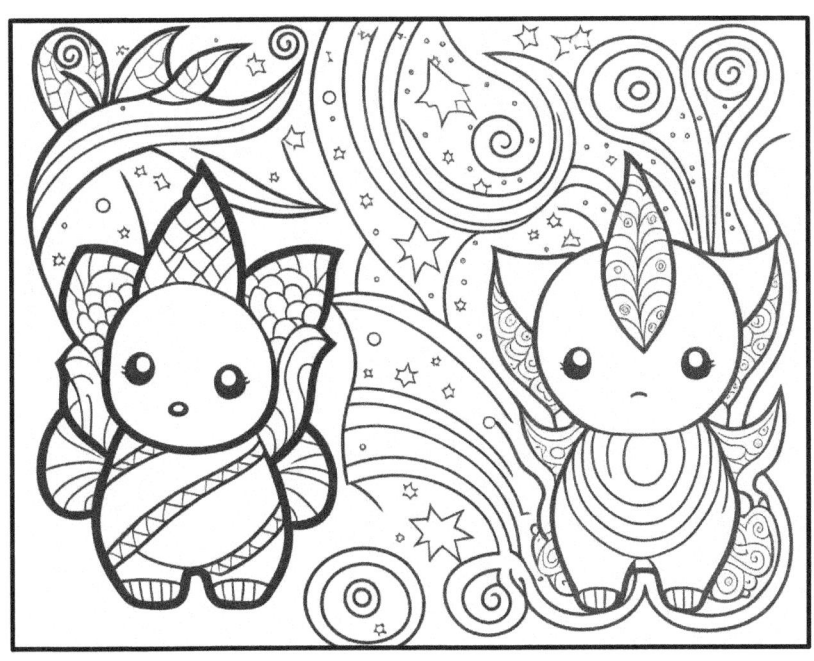

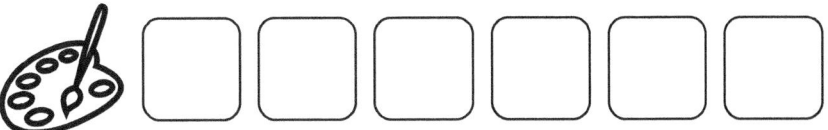

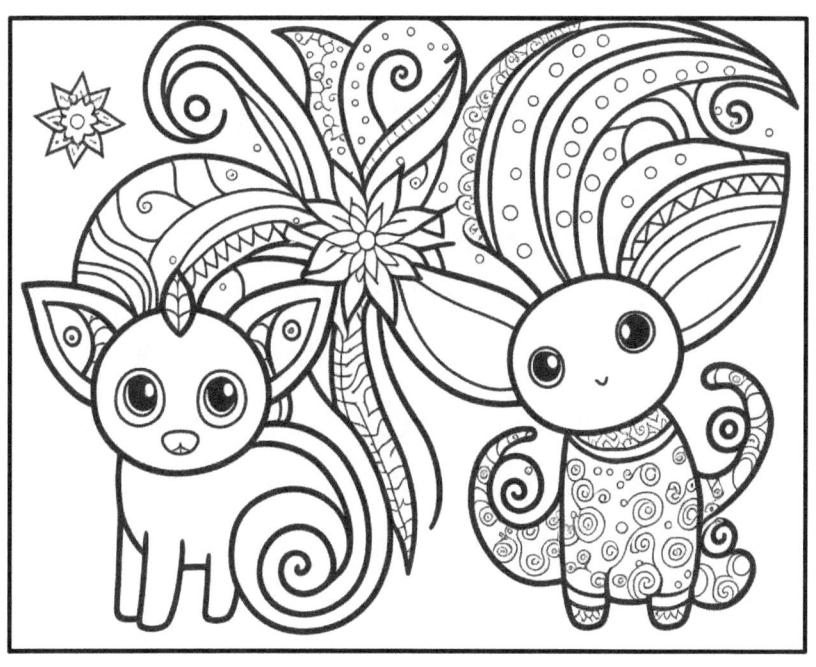

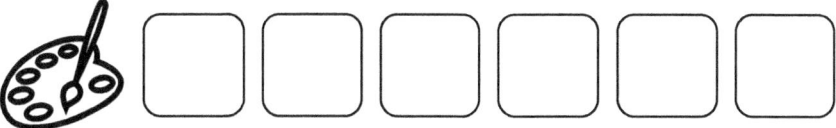

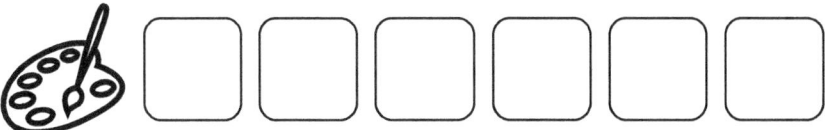

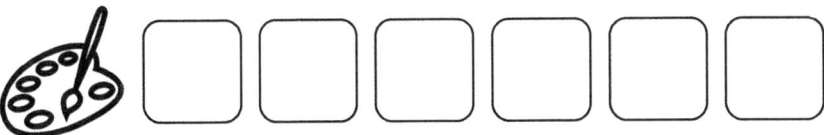

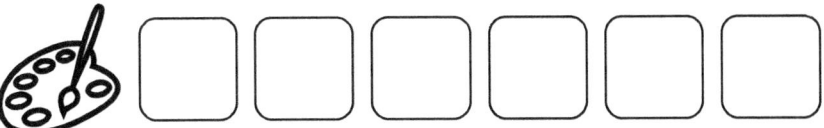

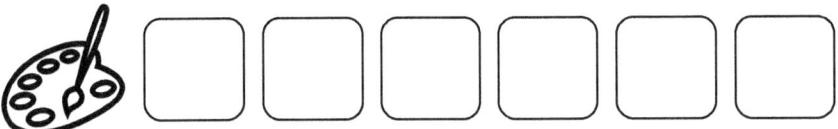

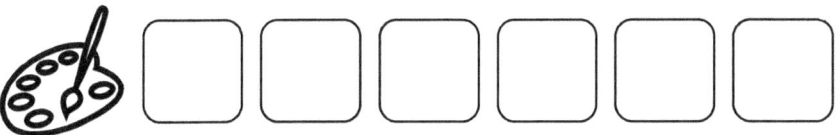

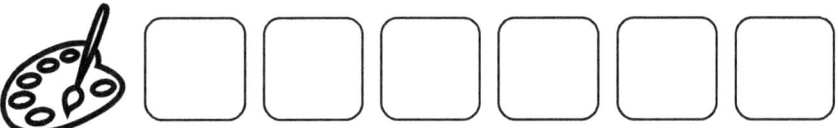

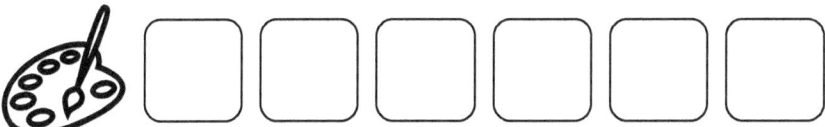

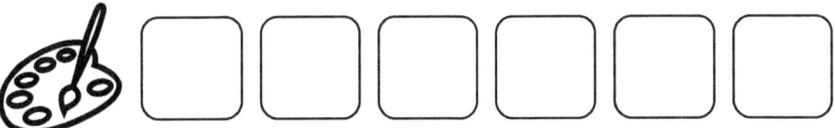

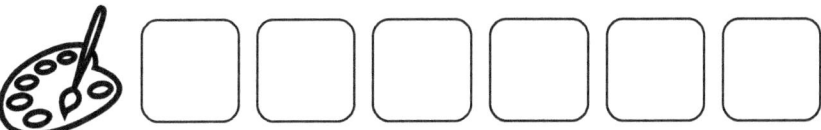

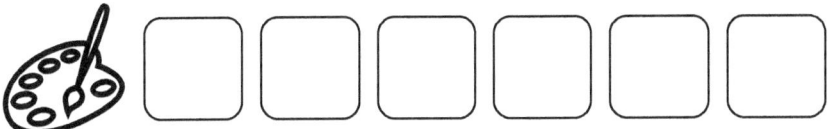

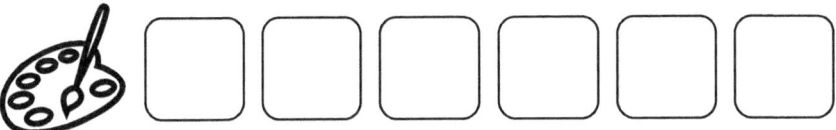

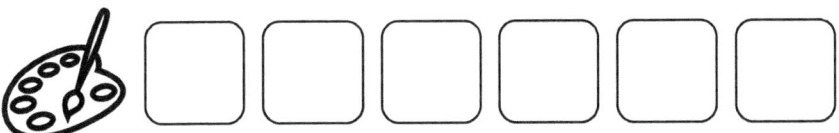

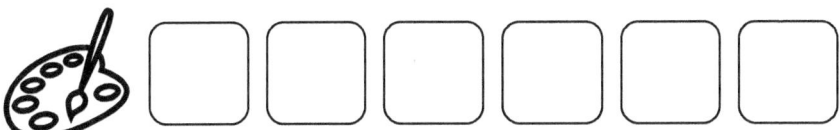

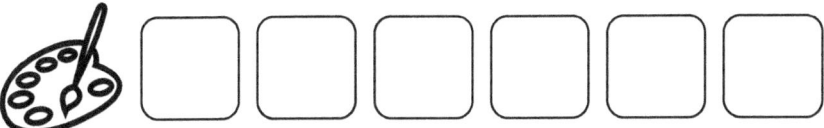

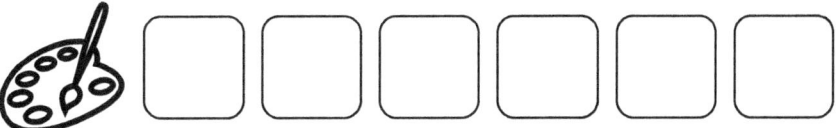

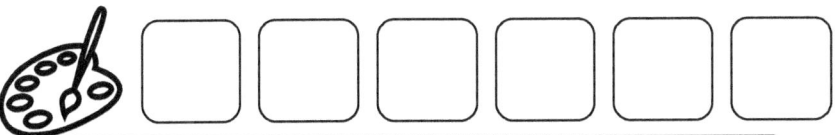

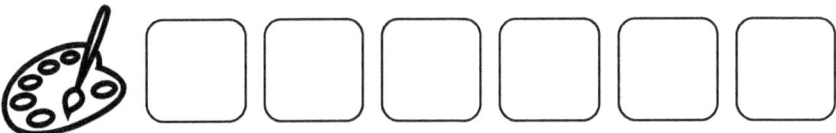

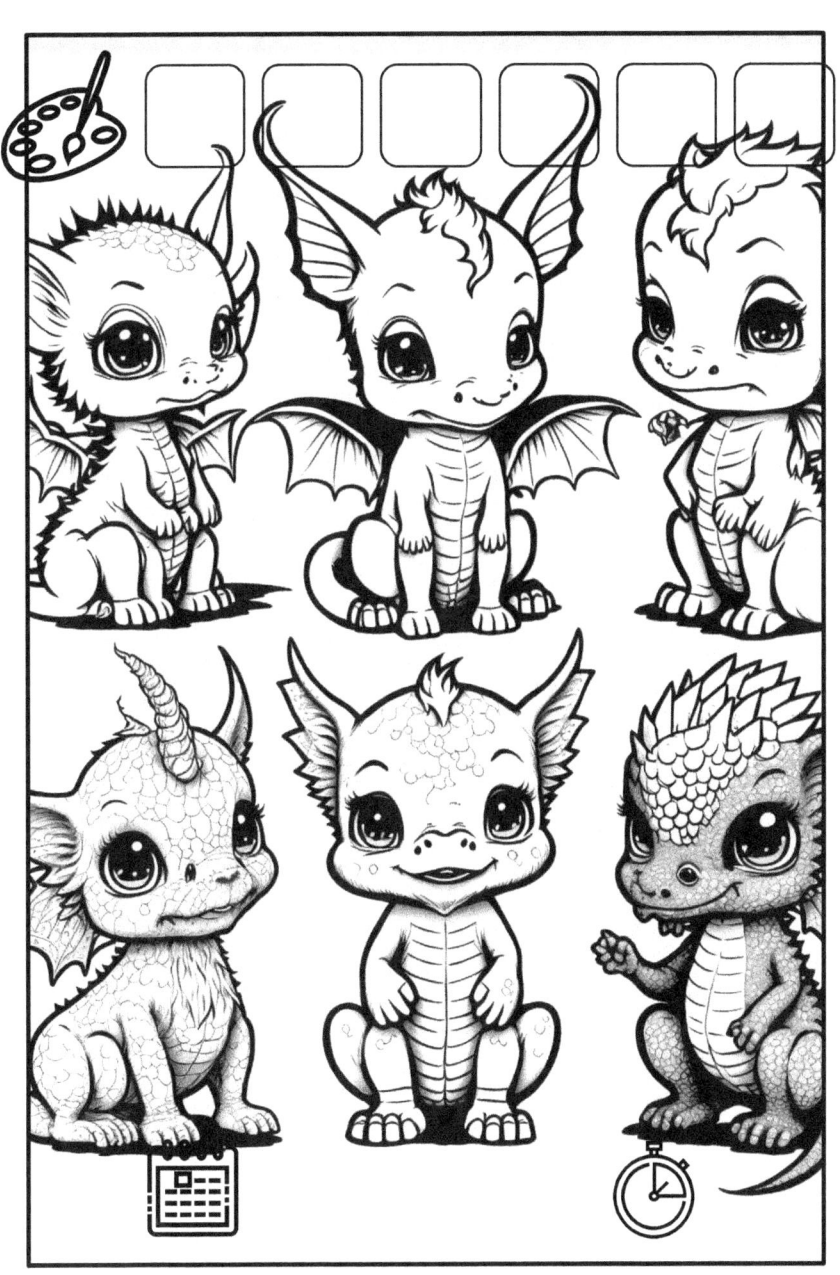

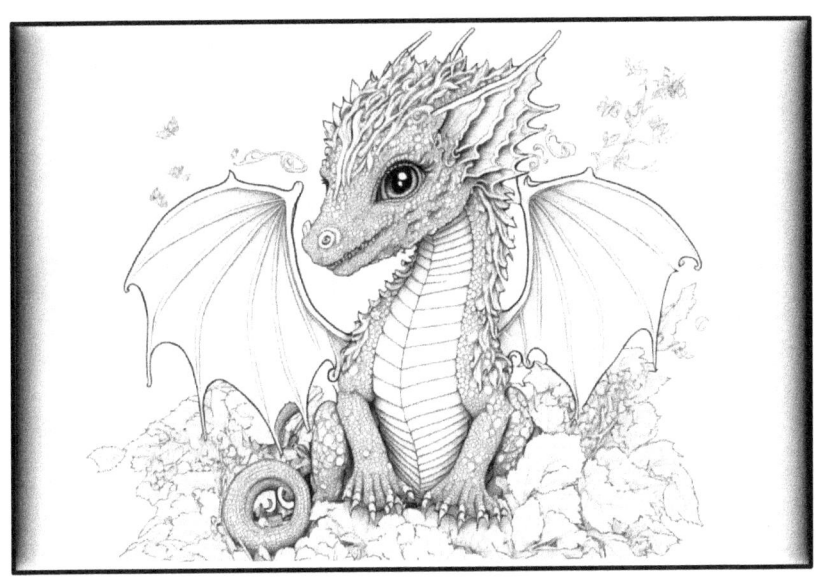

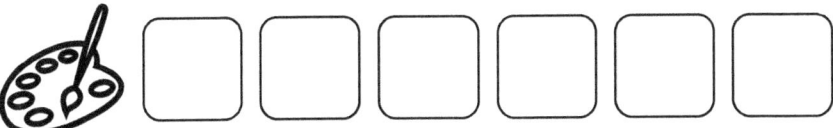

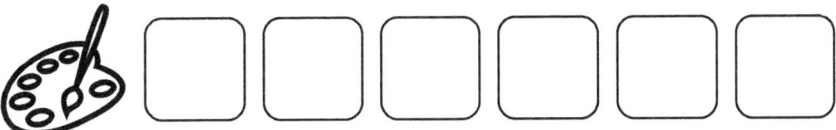

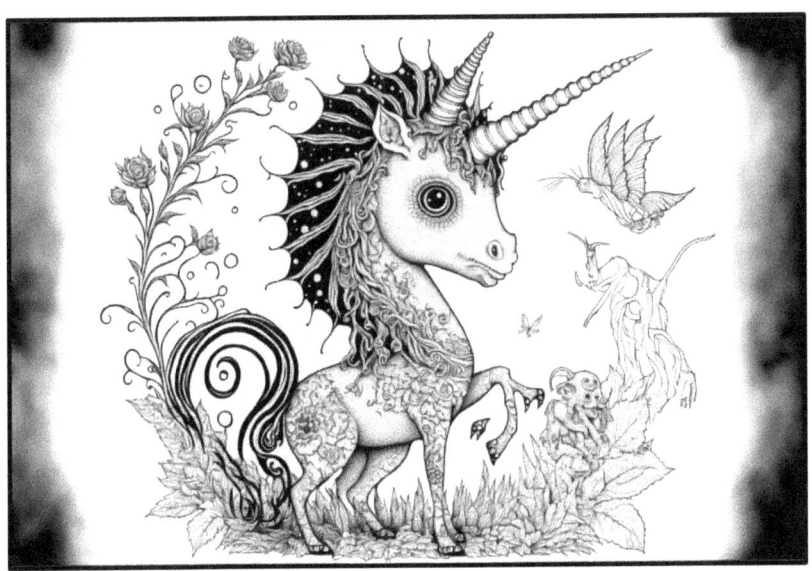

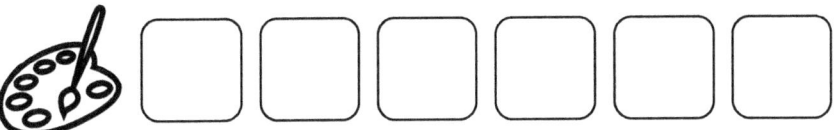

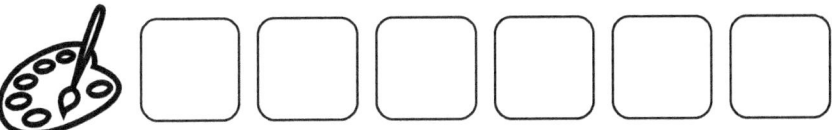

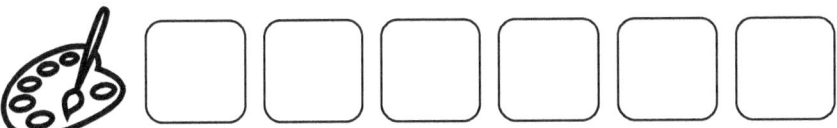

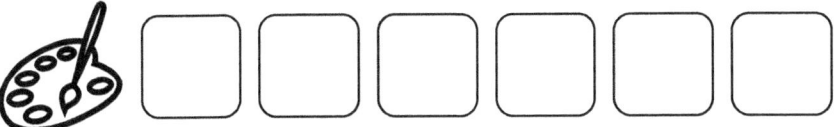

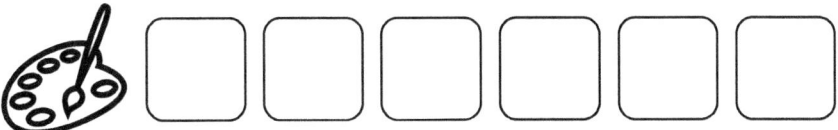

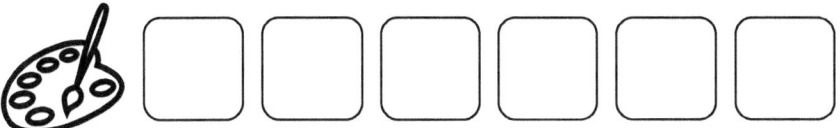

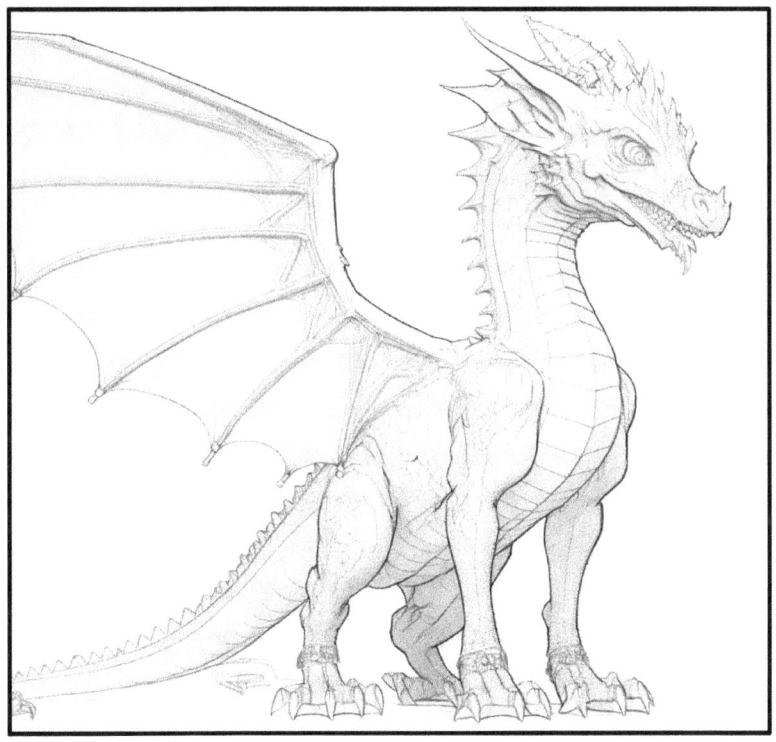

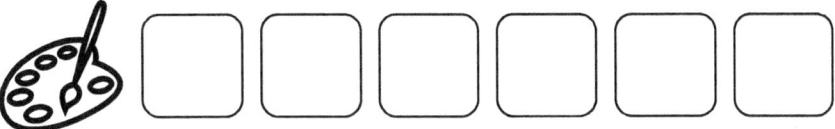

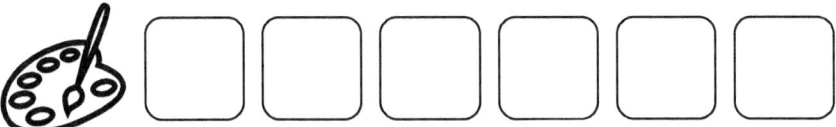

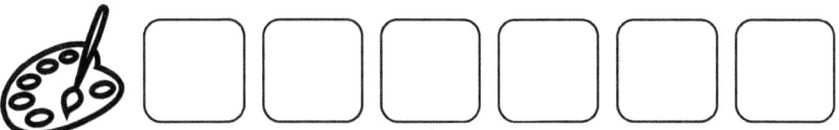

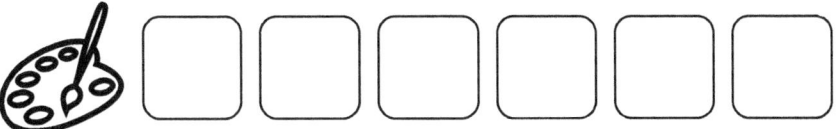

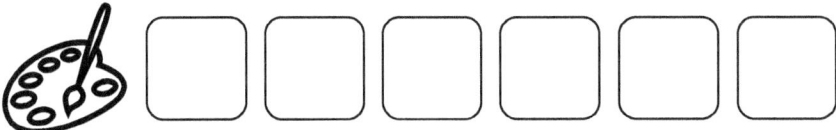

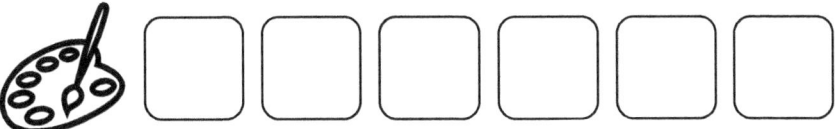

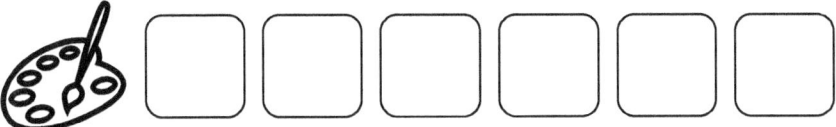

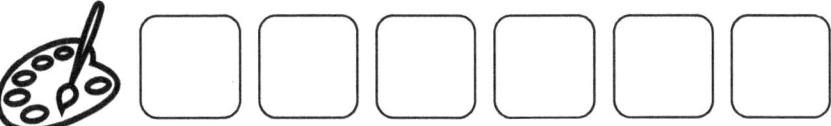

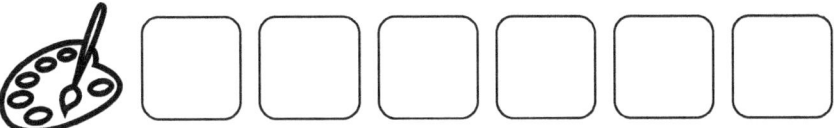

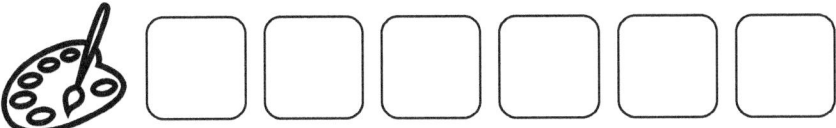

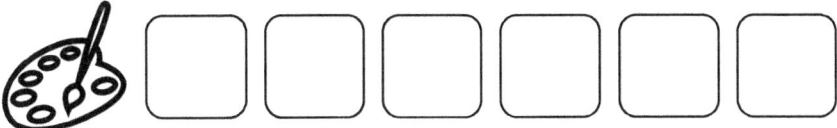

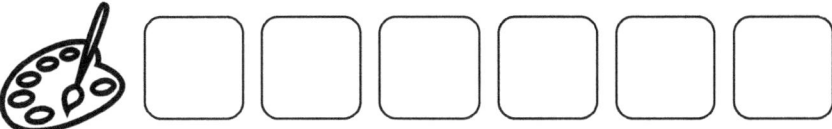

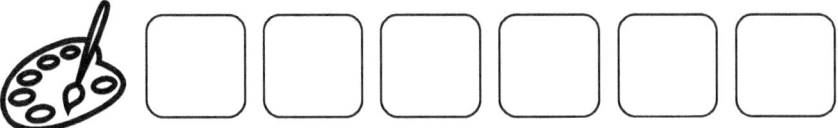

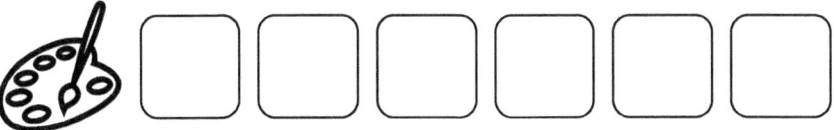

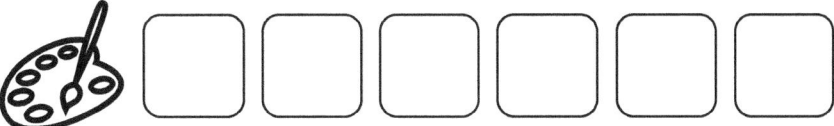

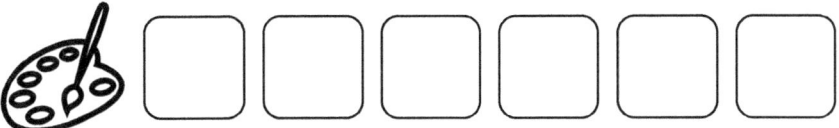

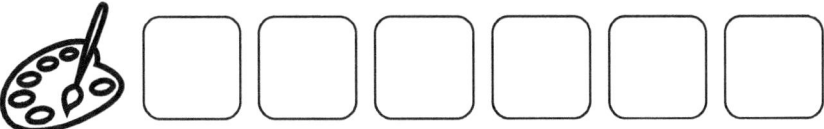

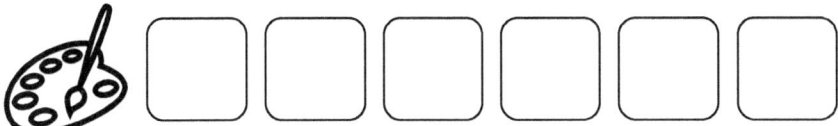

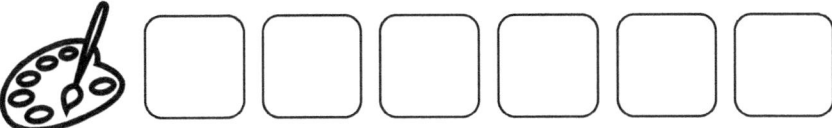

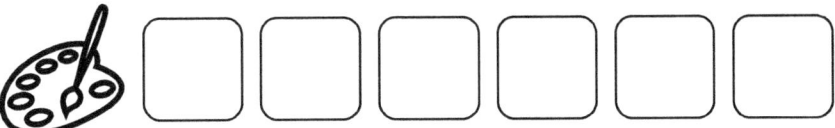

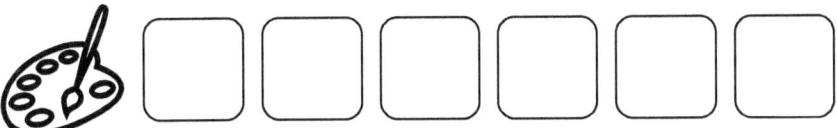

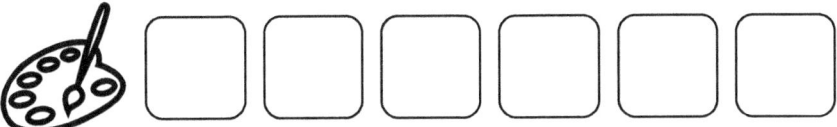

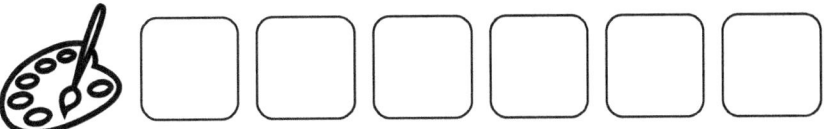

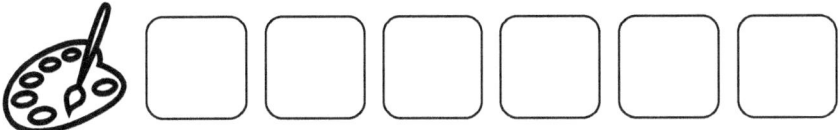

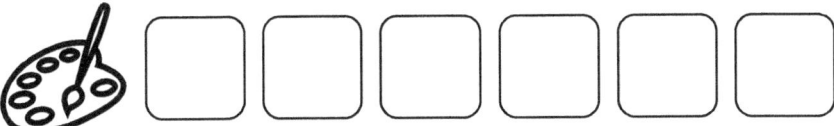

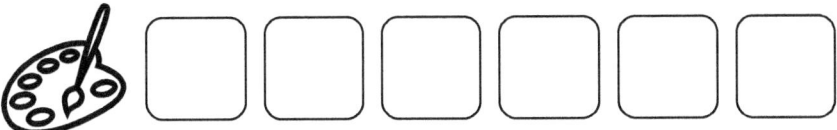

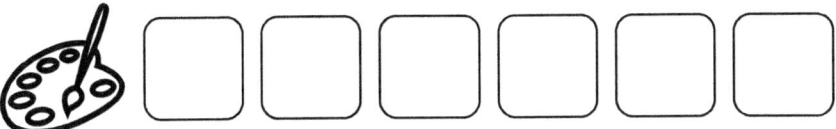

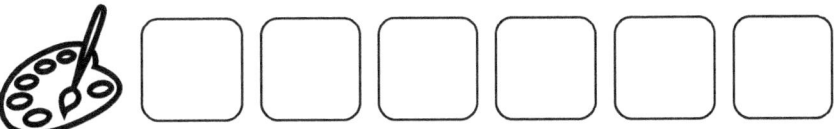

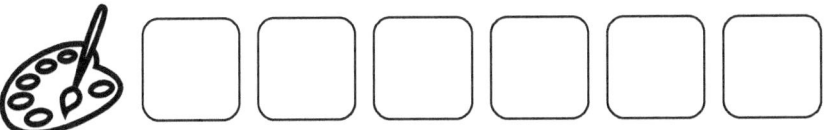

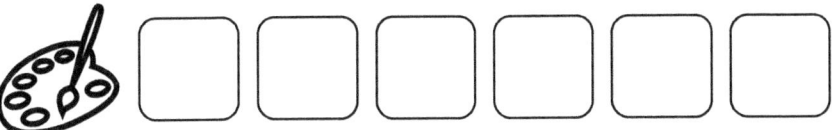

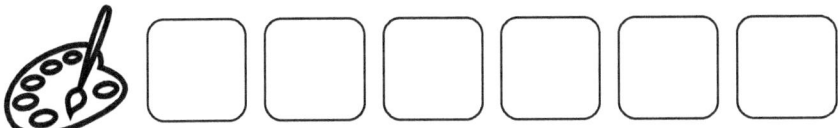

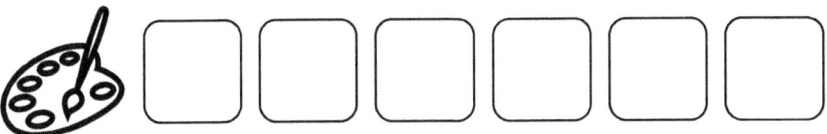

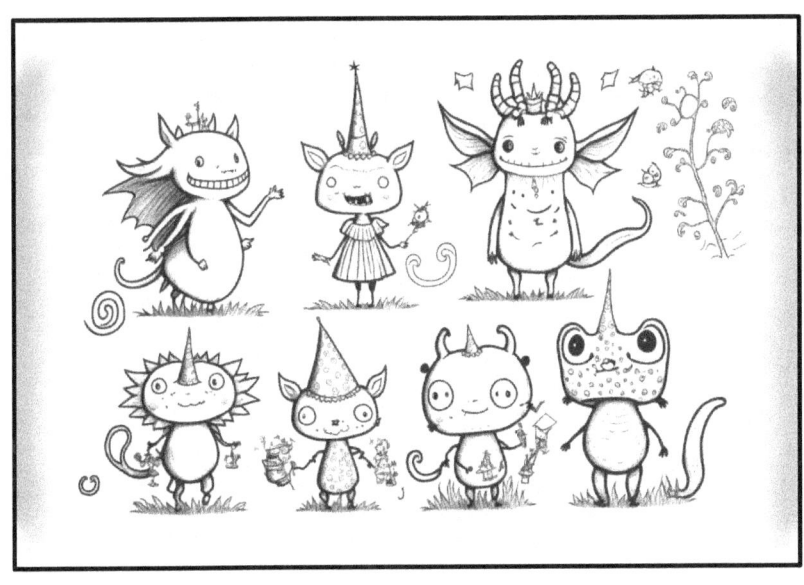

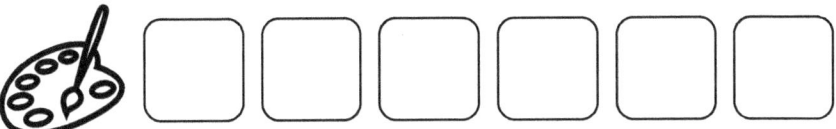

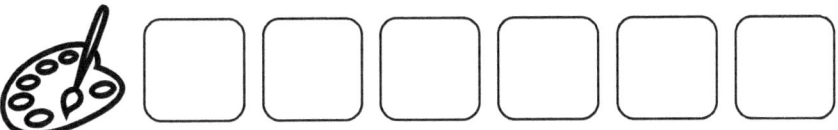

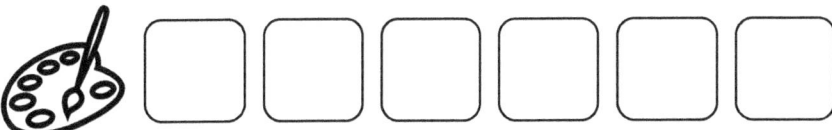

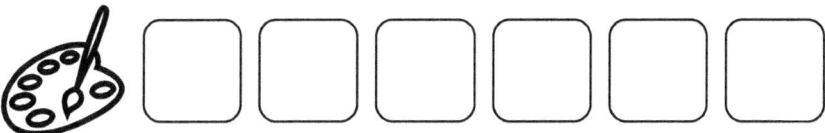

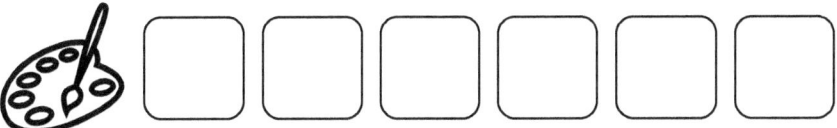

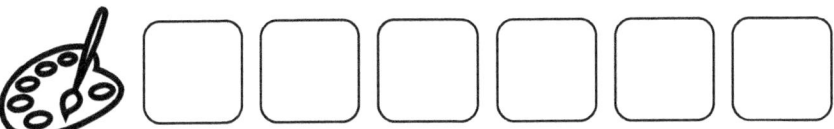

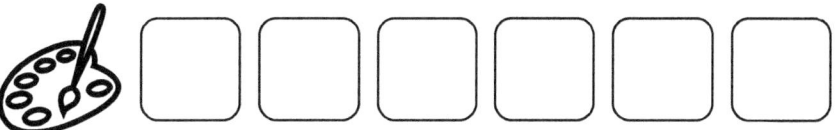

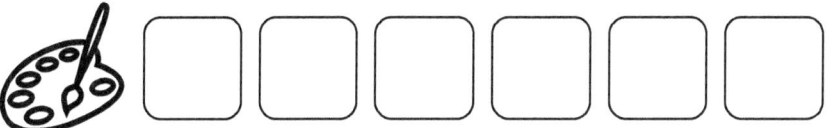

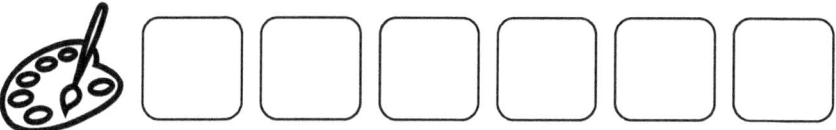

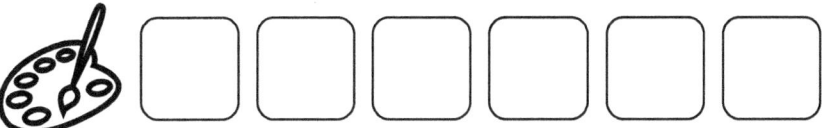